T0130112

Free the
SLAVES

Free the
SLAVES

Dawn Marie Eveland

iUniverse®

FREE THE SLAVES

iUniverse books may be ordered through booksellers or by contacting:

iUniverse
1663 Liberty Drive
Bloomington, IN 47403
www.iuniverse.com
1-800-Authors (1-800-288-4677)

ISBN: 978-1-5320-9393-7 (sc)
ISBN: 978-1-5320-9394-4 (e)

Library of Congress Control Number: 2020903392

Print information available on the last page.

iUniverse rev. date: 02/19/2020

CONTENTS

Prelude vii

Book 1   Unto You The Hero Is Come 1

Book 2   Discipleship 27

Book 3   Brothers And Sisters.......................................38

Book 4   Seeds Of Freedom...48

Book 5   Conclusion And Resolution 73

PRELUDE

About nine years ago I began seeing a movie playing in my head. I felt like I had started reading a book and was just following along wondering what's next? The very beginning however was dark and jarring emotionally. As a woman what I began to experience was empathy that comes from the shared bond of sisterhood-abuse in a brother's world. I took my laptop to my closet, sat on the floor and in the complete blackness of that small space; I let my hands unfold what my inner eyes and heart would behold.

Some parts were so close to me I typed through a veil of tears unable to read what my hands were transcribing to words. Some pages were so unrelentingly horrific that a couple of paragraphs was all I could suffer to type. I would escape the closet and weep seeking anything to divert my mind from that darkness. With every word there was suffering. I suffered first in my head watching then as it passed through my hands trembling and chokingly pushed on through until Book 1 was complete. During most of these deeply emotional sections of writing I felt like a free floating spirit able to step into the movie, feel it all around and even step into different people and feel them inside out, a fluidity of feelings and experiences from a multitude of perspectives. A great many other parts of the story were very detached like watching events in a theatre. The obscurity, time, and people of the story and jumping between perspectives until I felt time melted together as illusory as everything in this world, according to Einstein.

The other Books came later and in more freedom and light. Book 5 was written a full year after I had finished all the other sections except

2 which may be written shortly after this Prologue is complete. The Aquarian Gospel tells of Jesus life during the period of Book 2. I feel no compelling or urging to retell that story which is rich and full of lessons in perfection and the preparation for Christ to fulfill God's Holy will at the appointed time. I have chosen to include a couple modern perspectives on some parables of Christ as a description of the man Jesus as the student preparing for his life mission. Preparation is so key to the unfolding of all Holy events. A great deal of questions will be addressed in Book 5.

Before I share this story I will briefly share a couple short stories of my preparation to receive this vision. A full biography may be fascinating and fun but ultimately those bits of my life and preparation are better shared person to person as called to reveal insight and revelation for one seeking the path of perfection.

I was born Tammy, named by my father. My entire life my mother who wanted to name me Dawn would introduce me to people as, "Tammy, but if I had named her, she would have been called, "Dawn"." And as a child I remember cringing, thinking Dawn was such a lame hippie name (comic irony such an uptight kid would become a hippie mom;-)) and thankful my Dad won that minor battle. But as Shakespeare said, "what's in a name, that which we call a rose would smell as sweet…" I have since changed my perspective because there is great power in a name and particularly in the power to choose and give a name to something. The simple explanation to male dominance in Genesis is stated, ", and Adam named everything". As a direct result, Adam owned everything including his wife. And so Tammy which in Hebrew comes from the word 'tammim' meaning perfection was the badge and the crown I came into this world to seek. Birth order and a myriad of psychological, social and conditioning factors cemented the need for personal perfection in my daily life. I do not believe the need to be perfect was a conscious effort in the beginning. As time passed it grew to be the controlling task-master of my world keeping me locked in cycles of shame, disappointment, over-working excursion, destructive thought patterns and a general feeling of drowning and struggling every day.

A 10 year journey which took me dangerously close to death a few times found me in a mental space I had never experienced, the space of unconditional perfect love. And that single moment in my life changed my direction forever and completely. For when I experienced this powerful moment everything that was my life and all that I had known was changing, about to change and would profoundly change forever.

I awoke to find my life destroyed to the very foundation. I awoke to find myself more alone than I had every experienced. I awoke to find myself at a cross roads – die or live a completely new life. I chose to embrace the new and to demonstrate this new found vision of life; I was going to change my name. I had chosen a new name when I was 13 years old. I had suffered childhood abuse and at some point during this mental prison I decided to kill of the child, Tammy in me because I believed she was to blame for all my suffering. She was weak. She was needy. She was vulnerable and I could not have that soft, whiny, little girl in my way any longer. And since there were three 'Tammys' in my class, my new name came from taking "Tam" my nickname and adding the first letter of my last name, "E" to create TamE. I used this name for about a year until I just began writing Tame and everyone including my mom, family, school, church called me "Tame".

I felt a secret pleasure in a name which was such an oxymoronic expression since I was anything but tame. I had tried to change my name to Tame legally on several occasions in my life. Some circumstance always got in the way, like moving and losing the paperwork, having a baby, getting a divorce, starting University, the special signatures necessary to process and so on until I gave up the legal name change for the common acceptance that I was just 'Tame'.

My life, in a state of fallout and rebuilding required some powerful symbolic choices to acknowledge what was, what is now and what could be different about what is to come. My name change felt right; at last and so I would do it unto completion. I went online to the government name change docs and proceeded to print them except my printer ate the paper. Then my printer only printed every other page. Then my printer only printed every other line on some pages. I was furious;

book-marked the page, and went outside to rage. I stood in my back yard between aggressive whispering to mild shouting at the sky, at God. I was shaking with my fist in the air like a 3 year old showdown. I raged at God for every detail that seemed to fight me, resist and control me. I had tears when I exclaimed, "God, if you want me to change my name, you better give me one, because this is not working!"

Time went by, changed my web browser from Explorer to Chrome and lost my saved bookmarks with the name change docs. I was standing a short time later in my mother's kitchen. I mentioned to my mom and bonus dad, "so hey, I am finally going to change my name to Tame". My mother got a very typical look, tone and body language when she said, "well, I don't know why you want to do that, I would have given you a perfect name if I had named you, "DAWN"."

Well the utter silence of the Universe literally shouted in my head... peace. A peace and silent comforting, "Ah-Ha" washed over me. I was standing looking at my mom and entertaining a name I literally hated all my life. I was hearing it as if for the very first time, not as a curse but as a gift. I went home pondering the name and the feelings attached to that moment. And in a daze walking through my home I felt a calling.

I went downstairs to check on my daughter, five years old, non-verbal autistic angel. She was sitting at the computer and I went to see what she was playing or watching and it was the docs for name change from the government website. I just choked and stared at her and then the docs. How in the world did she call those government pages up on the screen? I have a completely different web browser. In a state of awe and wonder I turned the printer on and printed the pages all 13 of them, every page, every line and all perfectly readable.

That was Sunday night. Monday while my daughter was at school and my one year old son sleeping I decided to tackle the name change paperwork. I was finishing the paperwork when the phone rang and it was my daughter's principal from school requesting a meeting today. I arranged to come in before the end of school day and hung up. I proceeded to read the next page of the docs. The signatures that I had no idea how to get or find loomed before me. I needed a guarantor, lawyer, member of parliament and a list of people my simple world never plays with normally. The last name on the list was a principal of a school. I read that title and picked up the phone and called my daughter's principal and asked if she would sign my paperwork at our meeting today. She said, "Sure!".

The next special signature also popped out at me because since I had become a single mom I had been receiving help from the Member of Parliament's office to correct a mistake the government made with my child tax benefit. Once I became single the government had decided to investigate and cut off all funding until they could determine I was a single mom responsible for feeding and housing and caring for 2 young autistic children. I called the woman in the office who set me up with the right person and made an appointment to meet for signatures. Then I met with the principal for the final signature. I stood in front of the mailbox to deposit the documents. My mind was euphoric and fully aware that for 20 years I had tried to change my name to "Tame" and failed miserably. And now less than 24 hours after I received the new name, "Dawn" everything fell into place like dominos all prepared long before I knew I was even playing dominos.

I did not even have the $120 to pay for the name change yet. The woman in the government office calmed and assured me they do not withdraw the money until after all the paperwork is done in about 6 weeks which gave me time to get that money in the bank to cover that cheque.

And so my mother named me twice. Once in the womb but at birth I was not ready to receive that name. Then later after completing my journey I reached a fork in the road, one side was death the other a new life. Forever I am connected to God who prepared and trained me to be worthy of the name, Dawn. And I am connected to my mother who gave the name to me again when I asked God what that name should be.

And that story is the model of the last 10 years of my life. When I am thinking, feeling, speaking and doing what I am called to think, feel, say and do everything is already prepared and gracefully and easily accomplished. Anytime I go out on my own to do what I want, I fall and fail miserably. I came to realize that Jesus walked a path prepared. And each of us has a perfect path prepared perfectly and we know when we are walking it because it flows like rivers of love. In all things there is beauty, miracles and wonders when we are aligned with our purpose. The notion of Jesus' message of how he teaches Truth that brings rest finally had a home in my understanding. Life gets in the way of all that we are here to do until we remember who we came here to be.

Since I received my new name from God my life has forever changed. I began to study everything, every moment, every thought, every feeling. I woke everyday compelled to know who I am and why I am here and then be it fully. With this journey came visions, dreams, angels and miracles.

One dream that is the most important dream came to me to make clear to me what this world is and why it was created. I dreamed I was climbing a stair case. I was at the bottom. I jumped over the first step and began on the second to ascend to the top. At the top was a ceiling. Stairs that led to a solid ceiling and I stood at the top stair feeling the ceiling and searching for surely there must be a way past this blockade. I could hear and sense things happening on the other side. I needed to know what was happening on the other side of that wall. I called out to God, "God, who makes stairs that lead to nothing? God, what do I do?"

God answered you must go back down the stairs to the bottom and start over, because you missed the first step. And I did it on purpose. And that first step, for anyone who has been a support person or a person with addictions knows that first step is always, "SURRENDER". I came face to face with the realization that in this world there are only two choices. The two choices are temporary or eternal. I had climbed the stairs and learned everything of value to succeed in life but it was all temporary if I chose not to surrender my will to God. God taught me the Holy meaning of perfection on Earth. And in order for me to learn this thought pattern whereby anyone can succeed without acknowledging or including God at all, one must simply practice unto perfection. Like learning to solve a Rubik's cube or do a puzzle, or learn anything from walking to writing to cooking and cleaning, life is practice. If you know what God wants, expects and needs for personal joy in this life, simply repeat that unto perfection.

The only catch is without God all your perfect thinking is temporary. If you practice and succeed to perfect your thinking, which many do in part or in whole, you will create your dreams coming true and all manner of amazing experiences. But the value of your thinking without surrender to God, means that all that you say and do will only last as long as you live on Earth and as long as Earth exists. Imagine studying for a test and getting a 100% just to find out the teacher is not including that test in the final marks. In fact without belief in this classroom as a preparation for an eternal existence not only does your test not show up in the final marks but your name is erased from the class altogether. The people you made memories with will forget you ever existed because without a final grade, there can be no eternal progress.

To be perfect and negate God in your Earth life is to be a big fish in a very small and temporary pond. People who achieve incredible success in this world are like gifted children who Master University at age 10 with several degrees; but that is the limit and end of their value. They are little more than a wonder, marvel, superstar or savant in high school, but never making it to Post-Secondary education because of lack of belief in its existence. This world is a school meant to prepare us for eternal life, eternal value, and eternal missions. To choose temporary is like going to the movie version of your life, a mere reflection, a temporary foray with no lasting value past the cinema doors.

The problem is that the greatest power and asset to the anti-Christ today is religion. Atheists and Agnostics are better willing and able to perfect their thinking than persons relying on, looking to and following established religions. The reason is that atheists and agnostics simply choose to perfect their thinking for logical reasons: it works. They are not restrained, controlled or distracted by form and seek the depth of pure content. Religious people avoid perfecting their thinking, content, in order to follow instructions from books, people, traditions, prophets, priests, popes and other religious leaders who only teach form, illusion, and distractions from Truth. They fail to teach what Christ came to teach and continues to teach; which is that perfect thinking invites Holy Spirit to work perfectly always, in all ways regardless if the person is religious or atheist. God complies with perfect Truth from any and all persons equally. Obeying rules is man's idea to reach God and heaven. Thinking like God is the only way to reach God and heaven. The problem is the atheists think like God thinks, but failing to believe in God they lose their crown and the progress into eternity for all their work, time and passion unto perfection. Truly, this situation is the saddest of knowledge when the ones who excel miss the laurels and the credit into eternity gaining only the validation of perfect thinking temporarily on Earth.

When people talk about the anti-Christ they usually assign the label to behaviours or people who are contrary to the teachings of Christ, violent, destructive, despots. The people and behaviours are merely reflections of a thought process that negates the spiritual, the eternal, the Divine, the Source, Creator and God of all existence. The term anti-Christ as given by Peter in Revelation and Jesus is the adoption of thinking that negates the larger, vaster and more real existence in Spirit that makes this world necessary at all. To negate God and Spirit is to live a life under that ceiling at the top of the stairs always wondering what more could be out there but rejecting it just the same. The anti-Christ is a belief in a meaningless existence without any chance for progress beyond our own material bubble.

People of faith who achieve greatness in this world often feel compelled to turn around and help serve the weaker and vulnerable people of the world with charitable donations, thoughts, feelings and service because on some level they can feel the connection that binds us together. On a level of feeling they are intuitively connected to Spirit whether they ascribe to a religion or none at all. They walk in peace lifted and guided as equally as any who claim title and authority, for these new pioneers have walked alone with God long enough to stop relying on people. They walk in faith with a single eye and a body full of light. Unlike their atheist brothers and sisters they are working toward an eternal future in the school of Christ, not a temporary experience without meaning or eternal value.

These two personal stories of how I became Dawn and why I chose to go back to the beginning and start over are the two pieces of the puzzle that I feel compelled to share before delving into the journey of this vision story I received nine years ago. Writing this now almost exactly 10 years to the day when I filled out my name change documents is full of a feeling of release and completion. And completion is the true meaning of perfection on Earth.

At the completion of <u>Free the Slaves</u>, I had played with this story in my head wondering the same thing that I imagine others might wonder. Is it true? Is this a revelation? Is this a hoax or distraction? Is this, is this, is this….? What the heck is this story?

All my questions sent in prayer came back. Do not judge just learn. And when all my wondering and praying finally ceased, I began to learn. And that's how I came to be cleaning a toilet when all the answers to all my questions coalesced into perfect symmetry.

People have asked me if I am a prophet. I answer no. I have no desire to tell people what to do. I pray all will seek to know what God wants us to think, so all will feel what is necessary to be inspired, ready, and willing to do, say and be the person God has called and sent us here to be. The best parents live the Truth and are a light by example and so I desire to be like my Heavenly parents and live the Truth so that others may come to be free, be happy and be peaceful.

BOOK 1

Unto You The Hero Is Come

Many people think they know my story, but how can anyone know another person's story without knowing the heart and the mind of that person that created the story. One must feel the motivations, the very thoughts and feelings that drew experiences and situations into reality. All the set dressings, stages and characters are merely the myriad infinite details created by my mind and my heart's passions. The real story is the one I created before it actually happened. The story the world knows is only a shell of the life that was lived 2000 years ago.

I am writing today but retelling yesterday. Time distorts our stories, legends and myths because the people of today think and feel differently than the people of yesterday. In the time of my story, life was different than today. In my time all people, even the masters, were born slaves. In my time no one understands what I do and I must constantly explain ideas that no one can see but me. I was alone even though I spent much time surrounded by masses of people. In that time women were less than slaves; for the slaves, all men, still had some freedoms of choice and power in the minor aspects of life. Women were not slaves, they were possessions and tools. Men bought, sold, traded and used women as they would cattle and hammers. And more importantly I am a Jew. As a Jew in the time of Roman rule, I was a slave to slaves, an occupied people. Our histories were so savagely misunderstood by my own people and the outsiders too. And so I learned the greatest falsehood from my own family first. The falsehood that has tortured the hearts of most families since time began was the blame placed squarely on the backs and hearts of every woman as the bringer of evil, sin, the fall, and exclusion from God and paradise. Women were to blame for everything that was wrong in the world and a cohort with the Deceiver. I loved my mother and the split between that profound love and people's conditioned loathing, disgust and degradation of women tore at my heart daily. This split has torn at the hearts of all people so long as that blame has existed and persisted. If people knew how the game really began, forgiveness would be easy.

I understood the beginning before the beginning. I remember the time when the notion of the game first was born. My brother and I went to our Father each of us had a plan. My brother wanted to control the new ones. His plan was to program them all to do exactly what they were told. And for a time that was the way the world was. Nothing ever changed by choice but by necessity for the advancement of the game. Evolution was the program that dominated all living creatures and plants in this world, not free will, not choice. Every day was the same as the day before and there was no time. Adam named everything and therefore owned and controlled everything. For names are containers, prisons, of ownership. Then what? From the ownership comes attachment and power and from power comes imbalance as Adam had named everything he had all power. That imbalance could destroy the whole game if someone did not come to reveal the Truth to Adam and the world. I came to Father with a new plan. I explained that the world is perfect and beautiful, the most exquisite art, but it is dead if it never changes, expands, and teaches the Truth as the game is created to do. The perfect school is an interactive game that requires updating to progress unto perfection. There was not adequate opposition, no change, no choice and no action. I said to Father, "let us breath into the new ones who are free to think, feel, create and then choose unto learning. Let us give them a chance to be in control of their own moments, thoughts and feelings." And Father liked my plan and my role was set. I would live or die based on the merits of my plan. We all watched. The people at first strayed very little from the pre-set routine. Slowing over ages and ages of watching we saw one slight change. And then another.

We began to realize that there must be a catalyst for the change or they would just keep going and going day in and day out exactly as the day before without any advancement. We set challenges based on their choices. If they made a change that created positive expansion of the game it was rewarded and destructive changes had a painful or fearful consequences. And therein together Father, older brother and I, we dreamed the world that our Mother, the master feeler would cause all to live, experience and sustain for all people on Earth for all time through the creative power of feelings. We laid the foundation for the fall; we vowed to hold fast in heaven what they chose in the Mother's womb. Fear became like a plague that would sweep the globe in shifting patterns due to the shifting understanding of a few powerful new ones who seemed more curious and daring. These new ones became leaders of many people. The leaders although innovative at the beginning of their ascent began following the original programing of my older brother once in power, by enslaving the rest of Father and Mother's children under the law. We cheered and encouraged all who freely chose perfectly and then to patiently sustain those trapped in a fear cycle of programing or blind obedience. We wanted to see them learn from their mistakes because the passion to perfect is fueled by those bumps and bruises of life. All this was clear to me as baby in my mother's arms.

I, of course, knew and understood the teachings of Genesis, of Adam, of Eve and the shift from what we, as programed people, were into whom we were becoming, birth of Ego and free will. I knew that women were more sacred and I honoured them. I add this truth of my time to my story because the beginning of my consciousness was a tale of shame for my mother and for all women. For generations women have been shamed. Please do not judge my father or my mother for they were being the best of their own understanding. Children of my time came not in love, compassion, intimacy and grace but in defilement, shame, blame, pain, and obligation. Some thoughts and feelings are hard to digest but if you really want to know me you have to plunge deep down the rabbit hole with me into dark places. If you really want to receive the gift I came to offer the world than you must detach from all judgements and simply listen and live my story in your heart with me. Cry for us but do not hate us, we were when and who we were born to be. Be brave and follow me on my journey through my life as I fill in the details that the world of my time was not ready to receive; because they would never have understood it until now anyway.

Memory is a funny thing. Most people have fleeting flashes of memory of their infancy and childhood. I knew before I was born I was different. I knew because I remembered everything. And even after I traveled down that tunnel toward the white light, called life, I retained my memory in full. Thousands of years from my time most children will be like me, remembering. Our bodies are changing and our minds are the ones with the whips driving us ever forward. Thankfully, our hearts can sooth the scars of progress with compassion and forgiveness. Otherwise, we would be a lost cause and disappear with the legendary beasts of my ancestors. Remembering everything is a gift even a blessing; but it is also a burden, even at times a curse. Sometimes I vaguely wish I could forget like all the other people do, then I remember I chose to be here with this memory, with this body and with this purpose. I intend to accept that anointing with grace and ease. And now, I will share with you, all that I remember, good and bad they are a part of who I am, why I came to be. Who will take up my mantel and pass it on to the ones who are ready to receive, who has the eyes to see and the heart to feel the truth of all existence? And so my first memory is painful but necessary as first steps usually are.

"Oh come on Mary! Stop the bloody whimpering! Bad enough my father is making me marry you; don't play that religious piety girl routine with me. I know your father well enough to know that I am going too easy on you. You know the rules as well as I do. I won't take your precious virginity; god knows your mother probably checks you every day to make sure you are still pure as the lily. Just turn around, stand there and shut up and I will be done faster."

He used my mother like a garbage container. He spoke foul words to her. He cursed her for making him do nasty things to her. He cursed her for being so perfect. He cursed her because she was a woman and all mankind cursed the woman. Fear can turn into a powerful hatred that sees the one feared in a filthy light when it is the heart of the one seeing that is full of dark filth. Blaming my mother for all of his sins, all of his fears was the only way he could endure. She was his sacrificial lamb, as all woman of my time, were sacrificial lambs for the dark stains of man's fear and oppressive control.

Those were the first words I heard him say to my mother while I was yet in Spirit watching my parents-to-be. I had chosen her years ago. I had followed her blood line through her mother of course. And her mother was a treasure, but the time was not ripe so I waited and then the world knew Mary. I began watching her as an infant. My mother, Mary, was the perfect choice and I loved her when she was young. I knew even as a little girl she would be my mentor, my teacher, and my very own loving mother. I had delayed seeing him for as long as I was able. Joe was the man who would be my dark teacher and forge the path to freedom for me and my mother. Joe was a monster. We were delivered into freedom by the scorching and pounding of his pyre and anvil. Joe was my human father. We would be beaten and burned by his fear and from the ashes of that hell we were to be reborn. We were to be set free!

Mary loved learning. Her insatiable curiousity drew all sorts of unusual people to her. It seemed the more questions Mary had the more people arrived with the answers to all her queries. Her childhood home provided an unexpected bonus for a young slave girl. The wealthy master's daughter was the same age. She loved Mary's peaceful company and insisted she attend all her classes with her. They studied together learning math, literature, languages and theology. Mary excelled at the literature and theology. Her special gift was insight and depth of feeling. When Mary read anything she could feel the author, their motivation, their vision. She read everything like she was thinking it in her own mind and feeling it in her own body. The words became like vast stories all intertwined into a perfect mosaic of geometric infinity in pictures. In Mary's mind she saw pictures of the feelings, pictures of ideas and pictures that filled her mind with wonder, living pictures. Mary understood things that even the Rabbis did not understand. She would never tell them of course, but she could see exactly the point when their logic failed them. They misread and misunderstood vast passages of text from the Holy books. Quietly she absorbed lifetimes of wisdom from every person she met. She felt closer to the prophets of old than the Holy and arrogant and all too often ignorant teachers available to her at Synagogue.

As a humble and meek girl in a complex man owning men's world, Mary walked in faith steadfast as the North Star. Her father arranged a marriage with a man who although wealthy and full of expanding business potential was also known for drunken rages, fights, gambling debts and violence against the street girls he frequented. For her father the union was a very lucrative affair expanding his family business and a blood line that retained the blue stamp of approval from God. Her father announced to everyone after services of Joe and Mary's engagement. Mary smiled and stood very tall, her eyes clear and bright as they attempted to focus on some unimportant bit of nothing in the distance. She would escape as soon as she could find a retreat and collapse and weep at this most unfortunate surprise twist in her day. She pinched a little loose flesh with her nail to keep tears at bay and graciously shook the hands of every person that attended the services that day and thanking them for their warm wishes.

After duties she prepared for bed. She fell to her knees and pressing her face to the floor opened the flood gate. Gracious Creator Master, my God. I have read and understood. I have been tested and triumphantly maintained my love and light in peace for all in pure delight. I understand the words of Moses; I have practised the Wisdom of Solomon as you have set out for me. I have followed Your signs, listened to Your voice and heeded Your visions and stepped into the void with faith in Your power to carry me through to peace. And now I thank You for You have carried me knowing my faith is strong. You have lifted me over these tiny hills and now You are taking me to this even higher mountain because You believe in me. I love You and I seek You in all things. My life is a service to You and I am blessed to be used in Your service Great Lord. This man, Joe is vile and cruel and I shudder to think what a lifetime with that man could teach me, but willingly I go. If it is Your will that I serve this man as my husband, than humbly I accept and ask only the strength to do my best to serve lovingly. My thoughts have brought me here and as I surrender those of fear to You, now; so that I will create better anew. Please my God, continue to make my thoughts fitting to Your purpose and Your plan. And when I have served You faithfully and lovingly, please take me home to be with You my Loving Provider, my Sanctuary and my Guide.

And so Mary continued to grow in the grace of God. She grew in wisdom and she grew in practical knowledge and skills. And Mary grew into a woman and her betrothed who had not bothered to have a single conversation with her during all the years of their betrothal finally stepped to her side after a gathering and told her to meet him in the garden. Mary did as she was told and that was the first time he used her fleshy womanly thighs and buttocks to relieve his natural manly urges. A short time later, three months in fact, and yet several months before the intended wedding date a communication transpired in the form of very unique dreams for Joe and Mary.

Mary had yet, another of her regular intercessions with God's host of angels. She had become accustomed to the dreams that foretold certain key political and social situations and outcomes. She used this knowledge to help her family remain calm in God's Love to deliver them as God always did when they were strong in their faith. The dark dreams of Joe always left her torn in two. One part of her wanted to run screaming in the other direction from this monster. And yet another wiser more perfect part of her pitied the monster, even found love and forgiveness welling up from the very bowels of her being for this pitiful creature. She saw that he was devoid of love and any form of true joy in his life. Unable to save him, she would hold him in the dream and tell him he can be forgiven, he only has to try. She would wake from the dream and pray fervently for Joe's soul and his increased peace and joy. And then one night she awoke torn in two again.

The angel she had spoken to so many times before came to show her the pictures he would always use to explain the unexplainable. The pictures always made clear what words can never convey. The angel showed her holding a baby, a special baby. Her baby was wearing a crown that changed. It seemed the crown was the creation of thousands of crowns from holly leaves to gold and jewels it glinted and shone the life of billions of people in service to this all-crown of crowns. And the child was bright and alert like an adult trapped in a tiny body, the boy child looked into his mother's eyes and in his mind he said, Mother I have chosen you, since before you could speak in words. I have loved you and I will always love you. You will be my teacher and I will be your son. And I will continue the service that you have begun for our Great and Glorious Creator has a plan for me and you. Mother, go with Joe, name me and be my companion and my champion in life and I shall lay the road to freedom with my blood and my body for all.

That same night in a drunken stupor Joe had a dream. And the angel appeared to Joe. And the angel said, Joe, you are chosen by God to be the Father to Mary's son. Always remember this boy belongs to God and is born in service to God and God alone. If you will accept this great honour, marry your young fiancée, Mary who is already with child then you can be forgiven. You can find the answers that will end your life of suffering if you choose to find them. When Joe awoke he had chills and a feeling like being draped in a filmy gauzy material that sticks and carries on into the new day. He could not shake the voice, the vision or the deal. Throughout the day bits of conversation, scrolls, people would flash back memories of this all too real dream. The dream seemed to follow him around but always a few steps ahead.

When Mary awoke she ran to the pot and vomited. And sat down and stared up at a beam of sunlight, speckled with dust swirling in beautiful circles of patterned light. She sat and pondered the weight of the dream and the feel of her new vision of her own body. Suddenly her body was like a brand new thing to be learned and understood. My nipples are sore, I have to pee, I am pregnant. I am pregnant. I am pregnant. But I don't know how to get pregnant, I'm a virgin, no one told me what to do yet????

Mary suffered from public scrutiny for her obvious misdeeds. She was judged and she was the center of gossip and ridicule. She prayed for the souls of the ones who would spit on her and would call her names. A pity and love so great in Mary's heart enveloped those people in light and truth. The light of Mary made them fearful and so they lost interest and found that ignoring her was easier punishment for them than tormenting her. The pregnancy kept her busy in her constant bond with the growing child. She read to him every day. She read the scriptures and explained them all with pictures and felt the little soul in her womb respond and react to the wisdom she was conveying to his developing mind. She studied history and geography and foreign peoples and their religions and customs. She was enamoured of the Eastern peaceful mindset. And she longed to understand how they incorporate their faith into their daily life as she did with the books of Moses, her own history and Holy prophetic writings.

As the time progressed and she grew prepared to deliver, Joe barged in the door and announced they must move. They have debts to pay and taxes due. Pack a bag and be ready to leave when I return. He disappeared and she obeyed. She sat by the door, listening to God and practising her lessons until she drifted to sleep on the floor. He kicked her in the back when he walked through the door and shouted at her for being in his way. He rifled through some drawers and filled two satchels. With some meagre portions of food and wine they proceeded to their new home.

The travel was only bearable for Mary because she was floating in and out of consciousness. Pain, nausea, and random contractions plagued her all the way. She was so hungry and dehydrated. And Joe was angry and blamed her for everything. All day as long as she was awake he would continue this never ending rant about all the lists of faults and curses Mary brought to his life. He mocked her and he even used her for his own selfish needs. And through it all, in consciousness and in unconsciousness you could hear a faint whisper of a hum. She would sing a song of God's Perfect Love purring from Mary's dry and lazy mouth. Her body suffered with every passing moment. If she had been listening to Joe in her mind; she would have been bombed with all manner of maliciousness and violence, and yet, Mary's eyes reflected only peace. In those two tiny peep holes into her pure and gentle soul was a vision of paradise, of freedom and a new world. In those eyes was a mother's already unconditional love for the one being she didn't have to share with anyone yet. Her little son chose to be oblivious to the pain and discomfort of his mother and chose to only hear her song. Even over the dunes of hell with the devil himself, my mother created an oasis of peaceful abundance for me to ride like a king to my new land, new people and a new castle. And these dreams she shared with me full of vibrant colour and meticulous detail. These visions confirmed for me that every song was true. And even though I can look out and see hell and the devil, my mother taught me that to look in and find God who is the always the answer to any problem; that is the path of righteousness. And we rode like royals singing the psalms of David our Father.

Of course my mother was in labour for me the whole journey and never made a sound that resonated as anything but song. When we finally reached our new home father left us in an animal keep on the far side of town. He told Mary he would be back when he found a room. She gathered the straw and let the birthing process take over her. She surrendered her whole being to God and simply followed like a lamb to God's ever subtle instruction. The animals sensing the extraordinary event that unfolded before them drew close to offer warmth and support to this wholly unusual miracle. The tables turned as usually the human hands guided them through the process of birth now the animals saw a single human alone suffering and came to her aid. Mother Earth filled them with a longing to reciprocate for generations of care during similar challenging times. I knew what was happening outside and around me through my mother and as I became aware of the world with my own eyes I saw and felt a triple perspective all at once. Remembering who I was before I was in the womb, while I was in the womb and never losing sight of that singular self now still connected to my mother and seeing through her filters of reality I was born. I had eyes anew and was seeing yet a third unique vision of this moment, my own birth into a new reality. I was filled with awe. The world as I had known was wonderful and the world of my mother's was magical and now I was seeing a new world all my own to shape and connect. I felt so blessed to be alive in that first breath as my eyes opened and light flooded me like the opening of the Gates of Heaven.

My mother and I stared long into each other. Even after she had cut the cord I felt the thoughts she was thinking. I was at peace in her arms and warm night air full of smells and sounds was like the music of paradise. Then Joe returned, very drunk and unusually angry. He saw me staring at him knowing him inside and out. He turned stumbled and passed out in the straw. Mother sang softly of Love in all its magical forms. She sang of natural worlds and natural laws. She sang of wisdom and truth and in her songs I was trained in the ways of Light. Her song must have caught the attention of some workers in the field. They had brought the flock in to get provisions and gossip about the bright star streak they had been following each night in the fields. They were so busy looking up in the sky they thought the song was coming from heaven when they noticed the small keep and found my mother and me. The three men attended to me and mother. They offered her clean material and water and soap. They each took a turn holding me and chattering about their routines and dreams. Each mentioned how that star in the sky, streaking like that is a good omen and you little one are like a royal king in your little straw throne, don't let anyone tell you different.

They fed mother and helped secure us a room for the next night paying for a month in advance for us with food for mother. Mother had such a magical way about her; most people could sense it and always offered her wonderful blessings. Funny the three men didn't even notice my father passed out in the hay. Mother left word at the desk for someone to fetch him and bring him to the room after the workers had passed along on their flock duties.

As the spring herald of new beginnings streaked across the sky each night my mother would tell me stories of the stars and how they relate to how we create our own stories today. Mother made everyday life an adventure, an exploring learning living adventure and her passion for learning became my own. We were only in this town a short time and moved on staying with some cousins. I met my older cousin John and we shared in Spirit.

I stayed close to mother and she spoke to me constantly, quoting scriptures and teaching me my mother tongue and lessons. She prepared me to be me. The streak remained for a very long time. And where we were lodging we heard rumour that three wealthy men were looking for me. Their wealth bought them easy instruction to my dwelling and even as a toddler I saw something magical in their eyes. They gleamed with knowing and wisdom. Their words were few but so pure and powerful. They blessed me and my mother and offered expensive gifts. They said prayers and burned expensive oils. We ate luscious fruits and meats, honey and bread for kings that they had prepared to commune with us in fellowship. They spoke of a unity and a shift in human consciousness and evolution. They told my mother of things to come, things that filled us both with despair and understanding. They taught me some words to add to my lessons. They instructed my mother to take me to the Mountain and Valley people of the East when the time is right they will receive us. Faith and trust will bring you back together with us again and we will fellowship with all the company and hosts together.

After offering us blessings and a warning to leave this area and seek out Egyptian refuge for a time; they departed. Father returned 3 nights later declaring we must move immediately. As we packed our few items of necessity in the darkness of night we crept away from another home. I was not yet 2 years old but the words of those three masters replayed over and over again in my mind. I examined each word like it contained gold. I analyzed every look in the eyes, smile, nod and subtle physical communications. I spent every quiet moment unraveling the mystery of my magical visitors and how their words together with the teachings of my people created more interesting pictures in my head.

I saw connections between people and ideas. I saw patterns and I saw my place in the pattern. I was outside the pattern looking in and yet living in the pattern but not controlled by it like the others. I felt different and I knew it from the beginning. I remembered all the words spoken in private or among people for all those months inside my mother's soul, feeling, thinking, breathing with her. I remembered it all and had no words to explain to my mother or anyone else except I saw the world differently and I felt the world deeply and it made me feel very alone sometimes.

My father found most of the treasures left by the masters. He used the money as he deemed necessary. He had an unusual relationship with money. He could acquire money fast and vast amounts as if by magic but he used it up in riotous ways. He made poor choices, but Joe was a man who saw few examples of good choices when he was a developing boy. Joe was a master craftsman and a genius intellect combined with profound insecurity, shame and self-loathing. He was a man at war with himself and anyone near him lived in perpetual fall-out and friendly fire reality. Joe was a man who had the potential to be more but with only the experience and instruction of fear and control; he adapted very young to survival, always looking out for number one, because no one else was. Joe was a man who for all his socializing and gregarious boozed partying and gambling was very alone inside. He just didn't know how to make peace with himself at all, better to drown the bastard in wine than wine about feeling alone he would murmur into black outs.

Mary spent a great deal of time in her head. She had a wonderful imagination and her voracious curiousity only fed that passion farther and deeper. She blended her thinking throughout a day between a fantasy and analyzing that fantasy then cross referencing her understanding of the scriptures with this fantasy experience. Mary would synthesize the information to create more joyful experiences. All the other moments of her day were given fully in heart and soul to the care of her children and home including Joe. She was efficient and astute in everything she did. Daily chores were easy times to do simultaneous lessons in various verbal subjects like scriptures, criticisms and analysis. Mary was a practical dreamer and logical feeler. My mother was a bubble of joy and peace that drew all people to her to bask in her radiant being. I saw her sometimes and her eyes were sad. I knew that she too knew what it was to be so alone even when people were all around her.

And so we lived and we traveled and began anew the same old world we knew before in a new place. Our family grew and I was a brother learning to work with my hands with father's masterful training and artistry. I learned to care for young ones as my sister and brother came to this world with so many needs and all demanding immediate attention. I came to know what it was to offer myself in service to others in Love. I loved my father and I served him with all my attention and desire for perfection. I loved my mother and helped her manage our seemingly impossible and unmanageable life. And so by example I learned to follow the wind and keep no roots, I learned to laugh and love the tiniest glint of beauty and joy. I learned that the tasks of life can blind us to the beauty and joy that is all around us. I learned how to create a life of pain and misery from my father. And he also taught me to shine in mastery of a singular practice of a passion, his wood workmanship.

I learned the scriptures from mother and used every day as an opportunity to practise and understand the deeper meanings of those holy wise words. From my sister and brother I learned to see the world through eyes I had no understanding of, the world they knew was nothing like what I knew and remembered from my infancy and childhood. They taught me empathy for without their example pride and arrogance would have bread deep ignorance into my soul. I needed them as much as they needed me. In Spirit we were equal with mother and father and eachother.

I was prone to seek out people to discuss all these philosophical and spiritual teachings with people thereby creating more openings and perspectives for me to understand. I often wandered off to where the old men sat and debated great topics of ethics and esoteric mysteries. I would go to synagogue and listen until I was full of 'buts' and 'howevers'. I would engage the rabbis in discussion leaving them flustered and seeking a simple escape from the conversation. As I grew bigger there were more priests and rabbis inclined to listen to me.

My best friend and I met on one of those occasions where the priests were frustrated by me and shooed me out of the temple. He heard me speaking and followed me out to ask questions. And so began the only real friendship I ever had. He was a seeker and loved to study, being wealthy he was free to do so. He would bring his lessons to me the way my mother's friend did and share his wealthy power of education with me. I learned far more than my mother could ever teach me. The boys were free to explore any subject freely. Without limits I could devour more history and literature and sciences.

My first and only friend was also my first love. Until I met him my only passion was learning. I spent all my time studying and learning as I worked with my father and mother and siblings. I saw no person old or young who I could just be with as myself because that one person felt right. I felt free with him. He never expected me to be anything but who I am. If we spoke it was natural and when we would just sit in silence it was perfect. I had no logical reason for loving him. Being in his presence felt more real than stones and trees and all that money can bring. Sometimes he was my mentor and other times I was the teacher. Even though my understanding of philosophy and theology was far beyond his comprehension, his pure and simple wisdom and truth spoke to me like a sacred and holy teacher or angel might instruct me silently. He was patient and always kind. I understood the Truth of equality from him who being more ignorant of my purpose and studies unfolded perfect truth to me from a place of openness and innocence. He being wealthy never made me feel less for being poor and graciously accepted me as his equal too. He never asked for more than my company and acceptance. I was able to offer him the time and space we had to explore each other's humanity and unique individuality. In the dreams of my own future I see God using me to raise my friend from the dead and I wonder, "my God, what must I learn to be ready to serve You and my friend so powerfully?"

When father stumbled home in the dark announcing our imminent departure I for the first time felt loss. I knew that after we moved onto new lands and homes, the old was left and forgotten, and I knew I could never forget my best friend. I stood and for a moment felt a twinge of rebellion toward my father. I humbled my inner voice and remembered that my father is a mere servant of the path I am walking and to be angry with him for his service is to fear God my creator and to fear my own choices and my life path. I felt the lump in my throat swell; I felt the moist gush in my eyes and turned to obey my father against all the crying agony my body was suffering in that moment. I had never let myself become attached to anyone or anything. I saw the truth. I knew where my best energy belonged for me to become who I was born to be. This lesson of attachment to my beloved friend was one of the hardest for me to make peace with on this my journey not fully known.

My mother rescued me from my inner anguish. She had sensed this sudden move coming and had arranged to have letters sent to my friend from me through a local merchant. I would receive letters back and even though our bodies and voices were being ripped apart, our hearts could still sing in words on the page of our life shared only in the imagination of the reader. I was relieved to know that this one special bond would continue for now.

And so we arrived in our new territory. My father acquired a very wealthy employer who needed special and original designs made into a solid created form. The new employer was a family man as well and welcomed my brother, sister and I into his children's education system. He also set about to prepare me for Bar mitzvah, something my mother had been training me for as much as she was able until now. I enjoyed the extra studies because they kept me from missing my friend. And because I knew that this rite of passage would begin a new part of my journey. I had dreams to prepare me for the big events. And this was a dream that came from many perspectives on many occasions and dreams. Visions were coming to me more frequently and there was a sense of urgency for me to keep moving forward at a brisk pace towards the next threshold.

As the time grew closer for my examinations I spent more and more time at the synagogue speaking with the elders, priests, rabbis and other holy sects. I questioned everything and engaged in long debate and analysis of the scriptures. A couple weeks before my rite ceremony I lost track of time and stayed to examine the truths and dissect them with other critical minds too long, in fact, past the time for my father to return home to eat which I had never done before and never would again. I ran home and made it to the house out of breath but within eye sight of my father when he turned the corner hoping to catch me. That was the first night. The second time he saw the blur of my clothes drop to still before I made eye contact with him. He was angry but I was technically where I belonged. The third time I was not so lucky as he walked faster and made it to our threshold before I even realized I was late. In fact I was so consumed with a doctrinal debate that I did not notice until he was standing before me in the Synagogue with mother in tow.

He was beyond furious when I was not with my family to greet him at the door as we did every day. He tore through the streets with my mother at his heel and making a burning trail to the temple. He knew

I would be there, where else in all the world would I be. I was safe and quite content to continue my study and sharing of prophetic wisdom when my father barged in on the wise elders and me heatedly debating a sensitive issue about equality and the passing of the old traditions, a constant point of contention between myself and the elders. They sought to dissuade me of my point of view at every opportunity. They continually worked to convince my young mind to their solid truth that I could clearly see was smoke and mirrors, transparent as their minds to me.

My father composed himself instantly as if he was suddenly standing in the presence of God. His tone, his demeanor and words were like the man I only saw in church. This man would arrive shortly before the trek to the synagogue and would vanish on the way home. My mother humbly supporting her husband's stance and authority shadowed him as he asked why I was here, when they had looked everywhere for me for days. And I in matter of fact tone told them, where else could I possibly be? I knew they had searched nowhere but this one spot because there is no other place I would ever want to be. I left the synagogue with my father's large hand wrapped around the base of my neck. I walked the entire trip home like this and when we arrived at our door he took me past our home to the workshop. And he tied one of the ropes that dangled from the rafters to one arm and the other to my other arm. He suspended me off the floor and whipped me until I was unconscious. And he left me there until morning.

My father released me before dawn. Today was the beginning of Passover and although my father begrudgingly upheld only the high holidays, Passover he surrendered his entire soul only for a time, my father was a different man, for that sacred time. I was cleaned up and prepared for the rituals, feasts, ceremonies and celebrations. I watched my father in awe during Passover. He was a good man; somewhere inside of that shell was a soul that longed for redemption, salvation, and peace. All the rest of the year he lived a cycle of self destruction. His choices, words and actions would fill him with remorse and shame so he would drink to drown those feelings until desperation drove him to his knees for God's help. He would begin the day a new man and end it drunk and violent and full of shame and fear all over again. Passover was the only extended period of time when my father was home, sober and at peace. We all loved Passover for its spiritual significance in our lives and the lives of our ancestors. Secretly we loved it more because of my father's reprieve from his own personal hell. A hell that he carried like a coin in his pocket everywhere he was, his hell was at hand. At Passover we believed that one day father would just continue to be at peace forever and the hell he knew would pass away. We savoured every moment of Passover and prayed that it would never end.

As my father carefully helped me, I saw tenderness in him that was so rare and special I felt the gush in my eyes and reached for my nail. He would never permit me to cry. As a toddler, I crept into his workshop and scooped up a small child handful of tiny wooden nails. I kept one in a fold in my clothes and whenever my father's words or actions would choke me and flood my eyes, I would dig that nail into my flesh. A leg, arm, the pads and palms of my hands, I would dig and dig that nail until the sharp stinging pain turned to heat and the heat would grow. I would focus all of my mind on that burning heat, a heat so hot it burned all my feelings to dust and left only the empty emotionless memory. I purged my soul in the fire of that heat. I felt clear and free of the torture of failing my father. And as I watched his scarred muscly and vein covered callous hands straighten my vest and brush a stray hair from under my cap I clung to that nail, that pain, that heat. At the end of Passover I would perform my rites and like unto a man responsible for my thoughts and feelings, equal with my own father. I would be receiving the power, the gift and responsibility of free will. I would someday be as strong as he always seemed to be to me. I so wanted him to be proud of me.

This Passover was unlike any I had ever experienced. I was nearly past the threshold of innocent child to carrying the burden of choice now and already I could sense and see the change of the adult's attitudes toward me. As we remembered and honoured the salvation of our people I felt overwhelmed and overcome with vivid visions and strong emotions. My body was changing and my energy was rising. I felt a power growing in me in my understanding of truth and constant search for all God's wisdom. During this Passover I transformed in my mind and body so fast and sudden I could feel waves of energy and emotion pulse over me and through me when I focused intensely on God's love and purpose for my life.

I walked on water and flew through the air the couple of days following Passover. The high of that time together with the last two days to prepare before my rite of passage was beyond any stories I had ever heard of the smoking medicines, herbs and esoteric journeys of the Kabbalah Rabbis. I was living in a very real and tangible heavenly existence. The flow of energy was strong and the Spiritual communion and communication was pure and clear. I had vision after vision followed by brief states of euphoria. My father disappeared for those two days and mother let me indulge in the physical experience of Spiritual Rapture.

The day arrived and that morning my father returned somber in his drunken state. He cleaned and prepared without a sound or any attack of any minor infraction in his mind. He was deep in thought and we let him be. As a family we would travel together through the streets so everyone could see me, the boy walking toward my future with the first glimmer of man's power. As we turned the corner a man stopped us and asked if we would take his mare. He gave no reason; he said he felt he must give it to me as a gift of ascension. He scooped me up and placed me on the back of a lovely white mare, such a rare sight in our village. My father seemed proud and slightly disgruntled all at once. He wanted the honour for himself but recognized that my honour would also be his.

We arrived and the evening was full of wisdom and song. We danced and told stories. I met new people and reunited with family and friends that came from afar to join me this night of my ascension. My friend was there and my mother had kept it a surprise. I was as big as the whole world in my heart to have my mother and my best friend stand beside me in pride and love. I looked at my father often and felt pangs of loss. I even as a boy knew more than my father ever would and yet all I wanted was for him to look at me the way my mother and friend did, but he could not give what he did not have. With slow and easy grace I walked through that rite of passage. I passed and I became responsible for my own mind. I felt a great desire to take full responsibility for my every thought, feeling, word and deed consciously desiring to make new and different choices than I had witnessed in 12 years. I aimed for perfection in all things, even in the ability to forgive imperfection. I listened carefully to the admonitions of the rabbi and pondered my own unique foot print I would leave for the world. Will my foot print be everything I dream it can be? Redeemed and ascending all in a matter of three days, I felt like a king ready to face the world as a man.

My first day of responsibility was not what I had in mind for that day, but I must admit the thought and feeling had penetrated my body more than one time and I was guilty before the day even began. Everyone rose early because mother was taking my younger brother to meet cousins in the village next to ours to the North. My father had planned a day with me that was revealed moments after mother left the house. My sister was at home baking and walking the goods to various homes in the neighbourhood to make money for her dowry. Today being a widely celebrated pagan holiday, many homes would want fresh baked goods for unexpected guests. In the town to the South the masters had a small amphitheatre where the residents could revel and celebrate the pagan gods with pomp and circumstance. The larger villages and towns all were given by the masters: gladiators, animals and various performing specialties and delights for people to come together under a common umbrella of celebration and unity of Spirit, a most effective and powerful tool used by the masters indeed.

The town to the South was my father's plan. He believed my first day of responsibility should be spent experiencing a wide range of manly experiences, and what can be more manly than games of violence, gore, and depravity. My sister tended to her duties of the day and my father and I left to travel to the games of the pagan gods of fertility. My father explained nothing and said not one word on the journey. We arrived at the gates and entered the massive stone structure. I could see clearly mastery of stone that resembled perfection of human understanding of physics and engineering. We were as close as the slaves were allowed to be. Many of the people I saw at our level and above I had spoken to personally at Synagogue about these types of entertainments. I recognised almost every face, a few I had seen in dark shadows and corners of town I was unfamiliar but father knew well, no names just a certain look in the eye that revealed a life of misery. The men I knew very well I puzzled over and they felt my stare as they found more distant seats and or stared off into the distance at something unknown. I felt confused and wanted to speak to them but father sensing my direction and intent thrust me deeper into my seat and told me to, "sit straight and look forward, nothing to see around you".

My attention was solely focused on the area and action in the centre of the space. Naked or near naked women danced along the outer rim of the arena, circling the venue. In the center we watched two men at battle with a variety of weapons at their disposal. One man was large in every way, like a giant and the other smaller, faster and remarkably agile. Betting was taking place on who would draw first blood, knock first one down, or win the fight by killing his opponent. I was amazed at the muscle and physical prowess of each man. They each showed great skill and determination. I saw how they made certain complex actions seem simple like breathing; truly seasoned warriors both. In the end the small agile man of great cunning chopped the giants head off and carried it on a spear for the cheering crowds who threw flowers or images of goddesses at the champion.

The rim women drew to the middle as the cleanup slaves cleaned and set up slaves, set up. As they retreated to the rim once again a chained monstrous beast was brought in a cage and chained to a spike in the ground. Several other men were brought from four separate areas of the arena. They were to fight each other while attempting to stay safe from the beast who wanted to eat all four men. This battle went on for quite some time, only one had been slain and the beast had damaged two others. Small openings in the outer rim sent wild vicious dog like creatures out to snap and chase the remaining contestants. The beast killed two of these fast and furious little mutts. While the unharmed gladiator fought the small dog, his wounded adversary stabbed him in the back, and the beast clawed that one into a puddle of blood while the remaining gladiator with half eaten foot and one missing eye hobbled around the arena, champion.

The next scene required a large table. A young woman was led to the table blind folded. The blind was removed and the large doe eyes of a terrified girl darted around the space. A slave she stood naked, still, obedient always. The man laid her on her back on the table strapping her arms over her head and secure to the table so she could not move. Her legs dangled awkwardly off the table end as her torso was flush with the flat edge of one side. Her legs were taken one at a time and spread wide and strapped to the each corner of the table legs. Her trembling and laboured breathing was evident through all this preparation, even from my distant seat. She made no sound and seemed barely present in any way except body; graciously her mind was in some other place now. Two other men came out with buckets and proceeded to use large soft brushes to cover the girl's entire body in a semi-transparent oozing liquid that even from my seat when the wind caught it, smelled rancid. The smell was easily recognisable as the vaginal secretions of a female cow in heat.

I looked at my father and he looked like he was watching the birth of some wondrous and miraculous thing and not seeing at all what I was seeing. Then a sound and my heart sank and my gut retched and I closed my eyes as I heard the hoof beats of the rutting massive bull ox that was making its way to the overwhelming smell in the centre of the ring. My father's fist hit the side of my jaw, only hard enough to startle me to attention. "Open your eyes, now, be a man or I will drop you down and beat you unconscious in front of everyone!"

I opened my eyes and sought the nails; please help me find the nails. I need them. I saw that Bull Moose rape and rip that girl to pieces backed by the sound of cheers and squeals and laughter. I felt like I was losing consciousness and knowing that would mean pain and humiliation, I found my precious nails. I stuck one in my side of my body, full in and left it there. Then with the other nails I jabbed the first one into my hand between the palm and wrist in that bony space that draws a line between the hand and arm where I could hide the blood and scar under my tunic, then the other nail into the other sweet spot and back and forth digging, burying my pain and shame. I do not remember anything following that evil sight and I do not remember it ever ending, I just left my body the same way that girl did down there. I saw her and she saw me and in some other place, we held each other until she died and I was alone. I did not want to come back to my body and face my father, the arena and all those faces I knew from High Holidays and sacred sharing. And yet some force, some hand of infinite love, gently guided me back to my body and said, "Not yet, my son."

And so I returned more broken than any beating I had ever received. That sight filled me with pain in my soul, pain for all those men, for my father, the guards, clean up and set up crews, the masters and the pain grew and it grew. And then a new pain took over, a louder more profound more overwhelming and all-consuming pain that felt like the inside of my body was being pulled out and I was empty and vacant of all life except the feeling of pain. That new pain was the feeling of that girl and every girl who had ever been treated, thought of, looked at or believed to be an object and toy to terrorize, control and violate. I felt every woman and Everyman and their pain was in every cell of my body and my heart cried out to them all, help them, forgive them, they know not what they are doing. The nail in my side kept me from convulsing and vomiting on my father and the nails in each of my wrists kept me from letting tears and choking escape my eyes and mouth. The nails saved me from certain death.

We left for home shortly after that horrific act and walked home in silence. I could see from my father's pace and face he was seething. Something about today turned a switch on in his mind and began to poison what was left of my father. I could feel his fury nauseating me and sensing that his thoughts were filled with vile intent I stayed very alert for any sign I should act swiftly. I knew in my body that something was to happen and I was to be ready for anything.

When we saw home, I could tell he had no intention of going in and passed directly beside and behind to his workshop. My sister was gathering some tool we used to work with the baking fire inside. She had finished her baking and was preparing to make rounds around the town. I saw her skirts but not her and thought instantly I need to go to her, take her to her deliveries and keep her away from home until mother and James arrived later that day.

Before I could move to her direction I saw her skirts disappear from the edge of the building and heard her soft voice squeal and yelp like an animal pup. I ran. I saw him, ripping at her clothes and forcing her to the ground while thrashing his open hand back and forth across her face. She looked like a doll, not even alive and certainly not conscious. I did not think I was already prepared to act. I had dreamed this and I had thought what I would do and felt what I would do and followed the sequence of my own mind's plot without even in the present moment planning or trying. I ran in the side entrance, grabbed the first rope, the one my father had tied me to, a couple weeks ago the day before Passover. I scooped open the slip knot and like lightening dropped it over his head tightened the knot and ran full speed for the large nail on the wall. The force of my action pulled my father backwards and upwards instantly freeing my sister's tormented still body from his vile intent.

The rope tight and the knot in place I saw that the very tips of his toes still scrapped the floor enough for him to begin to work the rope with his hands. I jumped and landed with both hands and all my weight on the rope. His toes stopped steadying him and swung free from the ground a thumb distance away. If I relaxed even a little and let my weight rest on a piece of wood or tool, his toes would touch and his slow suffocation would ease. He would begin to methodically release himself from the strangling rope with his dead black eyes fixed on me. And so I held on and I hung on and I felt the blood run down my arms and lost all feeling in them in the process. How I longed for my precious nails to rescue me from the pain and so I cried to God, help me, please God help me help my sister and release my father from his living tormented existence in hell. Please God, give me strength. And so I repeated that prayer and began to recite all my verses I had memorized over the last 10 years. As in a trance chanting a mantra I recited and I recited and I hung on and I thought I would pass out and he would kill us both but some power flooded me every time I doubted and I hung on. He held on too, his hands giving him a quick short breath before dropping down again to suffocation.

The pain he endured every time he held his body up for a single breath was excruciating due to his injury in the shoulders suffered in a fight where he was dragged by an enraged horse. Since that fight he could no longer put his arms level with his head or above without severe pain even without any weight to hold. Only by the grace and power of Love could I look at him and love him even as he died hating me and seeing my hands do it. I didn't see the monster any more, I saw a broken boy who never really became a man on the inside. Rage had poisoned that boy's soul long before he even began his lessons in being a man. In those black murderous eyes I saw the face of the devil and what fear can create in a young fertile child's mind.

I do not know how many hours my father dangled before he finally stopped twitching and still I hung on. I feared he would return from the dead at any moment and I would be fighting my father's ghost forever. My hands ripped open, bloody and my arms colourless and numb I felt my hands begin to slip and as I began to pray again for strength I saw my mother's face and I let myself go in peace.

When I woke up I was in a wagon. My sister was tending to me and my mother and brother were in the front driving the donkey cart to our new home. My mother led by angels had returned early from her trip. She found me and Miriam and set about to begin the life she had been dreaming since before I was born. She touched my father's cheek, my sister told me and said a prayer, and tears fell from her eyes to his face and then turned and packed and left forever with all we could carry.

Since I was born my mother had worked as a midwife and been paid great sums of money from very wealthy masters over ten years. We had always assumed when my father took that money and we never saw it again that it had been gambled and gobbled up by prostitutes and taverns. My mother was delighted into laughing hysteria when packing the cart she found a secret storage compartment my father had hid the vast wealth, jewels, promissory notes from very reputable people, gold, expensive perfumes and spices. Our traveling expenses were all paid in full and our new life would be not only free but abundantly wealthy as well. As my mother told the story of her treasure find again and again on our journey East, I began to have more visions. There were still trials to be had, but life was new and our beginning was to be with a new people, a new country and new culture. The Wise rich men, who had found me when I was a young child, told my mother secrets and told her that when the time was right to travel to their sanctuary in the Eastern mountains to begin my training. At 12 years old, my Bar Mitzvah completed only days before I had finished my own cultural training. Now I was to learn a whole new way of looking at life, Holy Scriptures and my purpose that would expand and compound my understanding of all life and the game/school of Christ.

From the fire I was reborn a phoenix. I offered myself to the fire and the fire offered me life. I no longer feared any pain or death. My only living persisting fear that I sought to unravel and forgive was the fear formed of the young man in me. I murdered my own father, the man who gave me life. And so I surrendered the last remnant of my child Ego to God. The passion I had to know everything and see God only grew from this pain. My focus, determination and motivation was paramount and I had but one thought, feeling and goal, to know God, to see God and as Solomon to receive all the wisdom of God in my life. And so I continually prayed that my Heavenly father would purify me of my only fear that could distract me from my goal; that my earthly father would return to seek vengeance for my one and only fear. And I would die as he died slowly tortured and suffocated to death by mine own kin because of my own thoughts unto fearful feelings and the power of creation.

For the thing which I greatly feared is come upon me, and that which I was afraid of is come unto me. (Job 3:25)

BOOK 2

Discipleship

Mark 9:35; Mark 10:43-5: The greatest among people serves all the people.

As I moved to new lands and new study with my mother and siblings I began my time of discipleship. I actively sought any person who could teach me Truth. I learned the religions of the people we encountered. I over-laid my own mastery of Judaism over every other form of thought and faith. Once one aspect of life is mastered every other lesson and aspect is expanded by this mastered perspective. And so I translated the teachings of Buddha and Hinduism and other esoteric forms of thought and belief into my native understanding of Judaism. In the beginning my only thoughts were to know everything. As I absorbed the new cultures, religions, traditions, languages and people my perspective and understanding grew exponentially. Until I found myself as I once was in Israel standing in public squares and Holy buildings teaching my holy and eternal family.

For how can I know the Truth, the reason and path of happiness, peace, fulfillment and mastery without lovingly turning my mind and heart to my brother's and sister's journey of perfection? We are family. How can anyone be happy, fulfilled and peaceful knowing the family is broken? How can anyone be successful when the family struggles and suffers so powerfully, profoundly, and unnecessarily? How can I be like my Holy Father and ignore a Father's first love, his family? How can I be Christ and fail to teach my family how to be Christ too?

We are all equal in Spirit and only in this vast school of Earth are we separated into valuable and un-valuable. A family broken and divided needs healing. Since Adam turned his sons against each other unto murder, we have suffered brokenness and division. Human father's need to control invites the adversary to wreak havoc on the children of men. For every action there is an equal and opposite reaction. And without the controller there is no adversary. And without the controlling father there is no suffering children divided by envy and strife. On my journey to be as my Holy Father I learned first the foundational principle of free will. And no person no matter how well-intentioned heals or blesses another by means of control. Each student of Christ must choose the path of remembering. And as I practiced being a Light, a guide, a brother sharing the educational experience with all God's children I practiced ultimate perfection of serving without judging and loving without expecting. In the mind of every person are the pieces of our family puzzle. Even one missing piece is a horror to the vision to behold. As a family we can only win, if everyone wins. One lost brother or sister is the torture of all our souls united feeling the empty space where their light was created to shine with us for eternity. There is no place for competition and control in a family. And when competition and control exist, the family suffers globally and eternally.

PARABLE OF THE TALENTS
MATT 25:14-30...LUKE 19:11-27...ROM 12
STUDYING, LEARNING AND APPLYING TRUTH: different choices carry different blessings

A Modern Translation of the Parable of the Talents...Using the example of students in a class studying independently as a clear picture of how God blesses according to industry, passion and focus.

God's plan and God's will are set. What must happen to fulfill God's will and purpose happens at the precise moment when it must happen and not one millisecond before or after the predetermined moment. We cannot alter God's plan or God's will but we can use God's plan and God's will to increase our value and usefulness to that Holy unfolding destiny. Our focus demonstrates our perfect and efficient study towards mastery leading to freedom. That gift of freedom can be used however a student wishes to use it; but the manner in which a student uses their freedom determines the level and extent of the blessings returned by God from their charity offering of freedom.

Imagine a classroom where students are set to work individually on a reading assignment that requires some questions to be answered at the conclusion of the class. Each student reads according to their skill and ability determined largely by conditioning and genetics. Two students complete the reading significantly sooner than the rest of the class. They are given freedom. They have time now that is solely for their own passions expressed. One student finishes the reading, answers the questions and looks around the class. This student sees and knows that some of the other students are struggling with the passage and the understanding required to adequately answer the questions that follow. This student proceeds to go around the class offering their time, energy and understanding to those students who have diminished conditioned experiences to enhance independent learning. This student has mastered a lesson and now in a state of mastery offers self in service to their brothers and sisters in education.

Another student who also completes the assignment early has the same gift of freedom. This student grabs a favourite well-worn and read book, sketch book, or note pad for writing and delves into a favourite free time activity of perfecting a talent, passion or leisure activity. This student is diligent and polite. This student is content to work alone and improve self without much thought or consideration of anyone else who may benefit from this student's gifts, talents and wisdom. This student is an excellent student.

The last student is a student who struggles quietly, refuses help out of shame or fear. This student has gifts but they are buried beneath a weight of oppressive thinking and over reaction to an unstable and unpredictable environment. This student becomes apathetic as a result of their ignorance and may become a problem to other students by being disruptive and distracting. This student has a heart that screams for help but a mind that has too many big high walls to allow that cry to be heard. It takes a very special ear to hear the cries of the ones who are buried alive.

The first student also has favourite well-read book, sketch pad and activity to explore and expand perfection and mastery, but they reserve that time away from the people who need them. This first student goes about the class offering insight and in so doing gains more mastery and perfection. With each connection this student more perfectly sees and understands the questions that come at the end of the assignment. Through repetition of the material and the many perspectives of that material that each student offers when a connection is made to study together; this student rises extremely high in their ability to make grander connections in life. So this student is a blessing just for doing what is expected and by knowing the answers that are required, but this student is even more blessed because their service to others expands their own mastery and perfection.

The second student is a blessing just for having read and understood the material but the blessing stops there as this student will not expand beyond self. Their perspectives are narrow and their wisdom, vision and understanding is stunted by self-motivated pursuits of mastery alone. They are blinded to the power of connection and broader perspective of life and mastery. They have not come to be shepherds or servants but to expand self unto self. God uses their passions, skills, ambitions and talents to forward evolution. They may become very famous talented people but until the heart opens to those around their personal journey is still one of limited perspective and connection.

The last student has talent, has everything necessary for mastery but no ambition, no inspiration, no motivation because of a mind saturated in fear and limitation. Buried behind a wall of ignorance this student is the face of tomorrow's crime and punishment. This student is one of the lost ones who need more unconditional love and more time and energy but instead face a world of cold indifference and apathy to match their own shallow minds.

At the end of class the time to go over the questions arrives. The teacher represents God, who watches the story of the class reveal character and insight about each individual. The teacher will not change when or how the questions will be administered, like God's plan they are set and predetermined. The only freedoms in each student's development is determined first by how diligently and perfectly the student sets about to complete the individual assignment. Those students who goof off, chat and waste time are scrambling at the end to be ready for the test and often only barely succeed beyond the minimum requirements.

The students who are done quickly and perfectly are the first two students. They cannot change or alter the plan of the teacher, but by their wise use of their study time they have gained free time. They can become even more ready to succeed beyond their original capacity by their choices about how to best use that freedom. The mastery of the servant-student brings more blessings both to self, the entire class, and the teacher. The multiple perspectives gained by connection help this student to see deeper meaning and layers of wisdom that can only happen when minds connect and reveal new perspective enlarging original individual perspective to include multiple perspectives as God sees. The teacher witnesses their industry and service and bestows even more blessings above the blessing of increased perfection and insight. And so 10 talents become doubled again and again and the exponential blessings continue through a life of increased freedom, insight, joy, and peace.

The teacher may notice the self-absorbed student master and offer more opportunity to connect and serve but ultimately that student has fulfilled their duty and their freedom is their own to spend. This student with 5 talents and still offers a perspective to the larger class at the time of questions. Their blessings will also stay with them in life creating abundance and peace but only to the extent that an individual mind can conceive it.

The last student or the ones who are buried by self-destructive thinking patterns become a challenge for all people in society. They are dependent, weak, limited and lost. They are the ones who most need the light and spend the greatest amount of time and energy hiding from it.

These are the ones that the teacher came to save. The wise teacher uses and trains the first students to be brighter lights, better connectors, more perfect examples of inclusion, equality and respect. The lost ones need the first students, because like all prodigal children they need to have a beacon to draw them back home when finally their need for change is stronger than their fear of it.

You cannot change when the test will come. Sometimes you will not even know when the test will come. If every day you surrender your industry, passion and focus to God you will be blessed. Blessed with freedom and abundance and if you are wise enough to offer that gift back to God in service to others you will be exponentially blessed with the eyes and understanding of Christ, open and wise and free. For in this world, or school of Christ, all people chose to come here to remember who they are and why they chose to come here. Many are called; in fact every human that ever existed here is an only begotten child of God. For as there is only one of each person ever created in the whole universe for all of time, each person in existence is called to learn to understand and be Christ. For becoming Christ is remembering who you are, a child of God and serving the family of God as God, our Holy parent serves. We are each and every one called to be the first student to prepare for 1000 years of peace which requires everyone to be personally responsible for self, unto perfection to teach and serve all. The second student may become a person of great power, wealth and influence but if they fail to serve their fellow students, as Christ, then all their success is temporary having only value here in this temporary illusionary world. And when this world ends so too does their value. To continue into Eternity requires the belief and the service to the Eternal plans of God. God requires us to learn to love, teach and serve the family unto perfection so that each member can begin a family/world of their own as our Holy Parents have done here in this world school family event.

The Prodigal Child
Matt 21:28-32; Luke 15:11-32

Relationships are the key lessons of Truth and perfection. We are family and we learn through the family what we must to progress to be ready and worthy to serve the family. Our world is our immediate family but each of us on Earth are connected to people of the past and future who are also our eternal family. Our family is broken and imbalanced because our perspective and understanding of our heavenly family is broken and imbalanced. Our heavenly Father is present but mother's life, influence and offerings are ignored, erased and undervalued. How can children learn all the eternal lessons of life when one of the two vital teachers is never in class because she is rejected by Her students as a teacher?

When a child rebels from Father's plan, they begin a new kind of learning. The learning is by trial and error, correction and practice. This journey is full of hills, obstacles, hardships, adventures, pitfalls and pain. This journey is also full of revelation, rapture and unsurpassed perfect enlightenment. For in the hard journey come powerful learning, wisdom, and perspective. Empathy can grow as the connections with other lost children bring lessons in perspective and understanding.

Remember our heavenly Father is never angry, bitter, resentful of the child who leaves home to find their own way home. Father knows that journey all too well having made it in distant past with all the scars of wisdom to demonstrate the understanding of a Holy Father. Holy Father does not yell, threaten, manipulate, bribe or negotiate. Holy Father gives all that love requires and stands at the ready for the blessed event of that child's return to God's loving embrace. God waits patiently and lovingly for the wise child who having learned from experience what works and what does not work, what hurts and what heals, what brings joy and what creates misery and sorrow. A child in that intense classroom of "hard knox" is following the path of perfection that can only come from experience. God is not disappointed in the child just lovingly patient with their journey of choices. For in every situation there can only be one perfect choice. God being God knows all possible choices and knows exactly the one and only perfect choice in any and all given situations. God knows. The child wants to know but rejecting the answer handed to the child, the child seeks to know for self, for sure, for progress. And experience and practice are the best tools of progress this world has to offer. God never condemns or judges the child's need to know, to explore, to understand. God waits lovingly and patiently for perfect understanding to open the heart to healing and the mind to perfection so the child can return humble and open to trust the Father's wisdom. The child has gained wisdom in the practice and dance of life enough to recognize the skills, knowledge and mastery of Dad, at last. At the same time the children add their own distinct impression and expression of Truth.

The brother however does judge, does reject, does envy and resent the child who left home to experience and explore. The brother's perspective is limited and infantile. Lacking the courage and motivations to rise up and seek life outside the safe and consistent arms of Father and home, the child remains a child even unto old age. The human mind needs adversity, challenges, experiences, connections, and courage to expand unto the mind of Christ. And in this time of my life in a new land and people with my human father dead in a workshop back in the homeland, I experienced and explored everything. And the greatest blessing of mothers is their willingness to let their children be. And my mother let me be. I am the eldest and so I was free on many levels.

My discipleship in study would always be a part of me but now was the time of my life and experiences. And I was a young man ready to know it all, experience it all, personally. Being free from the control of my father meant I had no one to rebel against and so life was simply experiences inviting experiences, to practice inviting perfection. In my mother and my two younger siblings I had connection and home but no control and no competition. When I witnessed the competition in other families I focused with my whole soul to understand the broken and divided children of the other families where father's law was law. My mother made no laws; she wisely assessed each and every situation individually and addressed them with the same individual wisdom. How can a law apply equally and perfectly to infinite diversity in each individual at any given moment depending on the prevailing circumstances? My mother was like Solomon, the wise king, who made no laws but individual by individual helped people to find, understand and accept the Truth. The greatest error of Adam, Moses and all the Fathers of the past was their need to control the family with laws creating religion being the greatest of all failures of men. God gave Truth and man in weakness and fear made religion and later its hybrid modern government. If only my mother were considered by men of my time to be a human worthy to serve the family. Oh what a wonderful world we would know as a family united in peace and joy absent of all control, competition and laws.

God's justice and fairness is not measured the same as human justice and fairness. The reason for the split between human understanding and God's perfect justice lies in the limited capacity for humans to fully feel and engage in unconditional love which requires perfect freedom from control or competition and a mother to demonstrate. No matter what sin or mistake a person makes God's love is perfect, eternal and complete. Humans lack the capacity to see beyond mistakes to the soul that is a puzzle piece of a greater whole, a part of the Kingdom of God. Lacking that vision people choose to punish and exclude those who make mistakes instead of mourn the loss of the brother or sister who is missing from the Kingdom, from the family meal. God feels the loss of that soul deeply and profoundly and our choice to reject and exclude that soul makes God's pain more intense and protracted.

Every soul that is lost from the Kingdom is mourned by God and often rarely even acknowledged by human awareness. We barely bat an eye lash at the daily suffering of our brothers and sisters who live in war and poverty. We feel even less compassion for those souls who are so consumed with fear that their every choice brings pain and suffering to self and anyone along their path. We fail to see the thief, rapist and murderer as a brother and sister missing from the dinner table because of fear, shame, ignorance and apathy. To see them is a reminder of the tortured existence that is their daily thoughts and feelings. No one wants to look into the eyes of the criminally insane and acknowledge the brother and sister in need of healing. Exclusion and isolation are systems set up for a singular purpose to protect the "innocent" from the voice of God that says, there is your brother and sister, where is your compassion, your wisdom, your passion to bring him or her home. Where is your love for your eternal family?

Instead of making laws, we need examples, lights, education and patient loving wisdom in this school of Christ. As we are each practicing perfection to return home to our heavenly Father and Mother who we rejected and left to choose to come here. We each chose to leave home to come here to Earth and experience pain, suffering and loss in relation to pleasure, joy and gain in order to learn to appreciate our heavenly home that we left. How can we ever learn to be perfect as God without experiencing and knowing all that God knows?

Every human ever to exist is a prodigal child of God. To be in this Earth is to choose to leave the known presence of God. And then while we are here in this life-long boarding school we can choose to prepare to graduate and meet God with crowns or not. People can waste the experience judging brothers and sisters, who are the teachers sent by God to perfect. And while choosing to judge, condemn, control and compete, forever failing to see one's family at all, self-absorbed prodigal children, seeing no one but oneself, everywhere in everything. Solomon was not exaggerating when he spoke of the vanities of this reality.

We don't have to think about the ones we don't see. And we don't really know the names and faces of the many and we can say it is someone else's job to love them, forgive them and offer them the skills, tools and opportunities to know and love self and be united in the Kingdom of Heaven. Those excluded adults were once children and were lost down the cracks of religion and society that teaches blame, shame and punishment as the road to obedience unto happiness and freedom. Blind obedience is folly. There is no progress in blind obedience, no advancing of wisdom, knowledge and understanding. Blind obedience is for the smallest of children and has no place in an evolving Christ who with wisdom surrenders self unto God for love of the family. Obedience and wisdom are learned skills like everything else that must be brought to the mind through active lessons of mercy and grace. Trust in God may be blind because God is always perfect. Therefore obedience to God must be as perfect. And we come to know what God expects perfectly by trial and error, repentance, forgiveness, and renewed practice. We often confuse obedience to people as obedience to God and vice versa but Jesus and Joseph Smith demonstrate the need to obey God over any brother or sister. All human forms of obedience must flow through the wisdom of Christ for value and viability.

And so, as a prodigal child in this new land, I learned how to surrender by trial and error. I learned how to obey by faith and trust in God more by the validation of experience. I learned how to see and serve my human and holy family selflessly as my mother and heavenly Father taught me by example. For the Word is Love. Every utterance or action by a human is either a gift of love or a request for love. God being only Love, gives only Love and asks for nothing. For in all that a perfect parent will ever ask of a child is to be happy and loved. God makes no rules meant to control. God makes no comparisons meant to divide. Every word and action of God is a complete gift. Only people desire, seek, want, request, demand and take. God is not silent because of indifference or apathy. God's silence is only demonstration of a constant and perfected ready state of listening, loving and creating to bless the family. While people/children spend their thoughts every day on self, God offers every thought in love for the family always in all ways.

BOOK 3

Brothers And Sisters

Brother, we go to Jerusalem for Passover. Let it go, it has been decided since 21 years and nothing can turn us from our fate. Please find favour in your heart with me again and come with us to Jerusalem.

I see suffering and destruction in this plan, Teacher. I see how they conspire because of your celebrity. I see the hypocrisy in everything on both sides. Hypocrisy I am ill from what I see, even in you. Brother, I love you like no other. Since that woman stole your heart from me I sit along the sidelines watching, vigilant, serving the cause. Suicide, Brother, it is suicide to go to Jerusalem with the tensions between the Pharisees, Sadducees and Scribes and how they have set aside those contentions for a single unified purpose to undo you. They mean not just to kill you but to destroy all remnants of you from the minds of all people forever. They fear you more than the devil himself. Eradication of you is their only supreme and mighty God now and they worship the many heads of the devil beguiling all to their dark course. I tell you Brother, my Teacher. My friend, if you ever loved me, if you ever trusted me and sought me for truth I am that truth now….I tell you, my Beloved Holy Teacher, IT IS SUICIDE!

I reach for him and he pulls away. I step into his aura and just be in his space and feel his breathing begin to relax and the muscles to release and slowly he is my brother again. These passionate fits increase with his obsessive attention to them, stirring and stewing in his fears, ruminating in his loneliness the ghosts that drove him to my side, to serve and protect, to love and adore. "Oh brother, it is all set, we sit now and the pieces are in motion. No amount of protest will grant us a stay. We are here to begin what we sought to begin over three years ago. Freedom for our people, freedom for all people, it begins when we are free in our hearts and minds and will not let fear or people baptized in fear control our lives another moment."

He sobbed, Brother, you told me yourself. You confessed your father's murder to me. They will kill you for that you know.

Brother, you are the only one who knows the truth from my own lips.

What of your mother, sister, brother?

You, too, you have missed it completely. How is Perfect Truth to endure if I hand you roses and all you can receive is thorns. You are like them out there hungry even starved for truth and willing to accept anything without personal experience without seeking a perfect understanding. They seek only to be fed without a care on what they feed. They harvest nothing because they sow nothing. I stand there and say it is so and they believe me because they like me. None of them really knows anything more than an infant's ability to find a tit to suckle, but you my Brother who has walked with me are holding a crown of thorns.

Yes, I confessed to you my father's murder but you missed that part; too busy frolicking in fear and fantasy. Wake up, because the perfect rose, yes it has thorns but it is Divine perfection in symmetry, beauty, elegance, aroma and colour. That day before the Passover when I told you how as I was hung from the beams being beaten I oscillated between loving my fearful father and hating him with a depth of rage that created physical living pictures in my head of exactly the events played out less than two weeks later. I committed that murder in thought, feeling and vision; I smelled it like it was already real. Two weeks later without a single thought merely a habitual following of habit my body took over and did precisely what I had ordered it to do and there was nothing I could do to stop it because I was too afraid to stop it. If I had been true in Love and Light I could have saved my father and brought him into a new kind of life, a life of peace and forgiveness. My fear kept me from saving my father from my own murderous creation. That internal creation, my brother, my thoughts unto feelings unto creation was my sin. I ask you now, do you understand the perfect symmetry of which I speak? I believe you will come and you will be with me in Jerusalem, my brother. And I reached out my hand, he took it and our hands wrapped around each other's forearms. A slight turn and release and he was gone. I did not see him again until Jerusalem.

I dreamed it all again. It keeps returning to where ever I leave off from the last dream time and goes from beginning to end in fragments of time. When I was a child the dreams would trouble me, but now I just walk through them like an outside observer witnessing the scenes passively and calmly seeing all aspects at once. This morning we arrive in Jerusalem and I dreamed of the donkey and colt again. I will send a few to go retrieve the specially selected beasts to fulfill their purpose and the prophecy.

And now let us unite our hearts and minds and bless this endeavour. We all have passed through the fire and walk in faith according to our destiny and the fate we have created. Let us be thankful to God for our journey, our path and our purpose. Like this ass and colt we each have a special duty and when we fulfill in it in joy and gratitude we are more light and more powerful in our being. Brothers! This journey, this day is a beginning of a new and very old story and like every story it will have its twists and surprises for you to traverse without me to help and guide you through to its proper resolution. I tell you now I have seen this day a thousand times and I have felt its unfolding in my heart like the rose before the sun, my life too will wilt and pass away. I ask you all to remember the smell of my blossom, the touch of my satin and the glory of my colour as you go forth on your own personal journeys that I have laid the foundation for with my body, my breath and my passion for my people. Continue what I have begun, stand strong and let the Love of God be your only guide, your touchstone and your nourishment. All else in this world will pass away but God is Love and God's Love is eternal and infinite and in God's love you will be blessed. Any word that is meant to mislead you or take you from peace return only to God's Love and all is immediately revealed and you are delivered into pure knowledge and wisdom. If any word, any deed, any being resists or rejects God is Love, they are doomed to the fire of hell, which is the ignorance that allows a soul to choose repeat fearful painful creations until they repent and return to Source, Love, God. The Buddhist masters call this state 'Duhkha", to be perpetually stuck in a lesson of perfection. Even for the infant mobs who suck up my words, so long as they hold fast to the singular truth of all existence that God is love, that love is all that exists and our existence in the Kingdom of heaven is solely determined by our love for self, each other and all creation.

Let us go now, my time has come and it is now.

I had avoided this one place most of my adult life. I had avoided the home that I fled as a child. And now compelled I go. I feel in my soul that no matter what path I take whether my eyes be open or closed even if I had to walk around the world I will go to Jerusalem. If I were to turn my back and walk the other direction like a mystical illusion I would forever be taken back to this place and no other place in our world would accept me. I am where I belong. In my mind I kept replaying this monologue of reassurance. This monologue of commitment to what I have created and what I am willing to endure for Love, for God, for my redemption.

From a distance I can see the people, feel the commotion and the energy of light ripping and swirling en masse, like walking into a sand storm made only of light. The light thrusts itself at me and through me and all around me and I am lifted and caressed and plunged into a light ecstasy. I have dreamed awake and in sleep of people, masses of people touching me, shouting and crying my name and I have lived those dreams but this, Oh My God, this intensity, this overwhelming energy that is like all the hosts of heaven dancing in colours I have never seen before this day. I am emotionally compromised to see such fervor and excitement at my presence and my name. My chest is pouring and my head is swooning in love and passion for these people. I am in awe of them as much as they seem to be in awe of me. I am laid bare, naked in the glory of their enthusiasm for my coming. I see the branches and I hear the voices and I am exalted like a king, glorified with crown and sceptre. With all the experiences I have had of worship and praise, this day, this moment, these people are greater than all of them combined because this is my home and these are my people and I have come for them. My heart sang in swelling shouts, "I LOVE YOU, I LOVE YOU ALL!" Again and again my head exploded like fire into the stars and my heart sang, "I LOVE YOU, I LOVE YOU ALL!"

When fatigue and necessity took people to their homes we finally settled into our rooms. We were all aglow. Not one of us could sleep for the elation was paramount. Our bodies sailed that night on an ocean of stars we sat and watched the heavens in silent rapture. All of the glory of creation and our place in its evolution was laid before my brothers in a way they had never experienced before this day. I finally shared with them a small taste of my inner world, they saw it before today but now they could feel it, for real in their own creating minds and hearts and they were transformed as much as I.

The trepidation I had felt before leaving and on the journey itself was replaced by pure surrender. I floated that night with my creator and I felt home on many levels. I saw into the future only the glory of what was to unfold from our journey. I was completely blind to all that was less than heavenly perfection, in a subjective sence. Encapsulated in pure power and pure joy, I felt that the pain that was to come seemed only a speck of nothingness in comparison to this pure high exalted being-ness. I was instantly transported back to my bar mitzvah. I remember the elation of a boy passing the threshold to new life and I was there again only bigger, bolder, brighter.

The threshold I passed through today was of a size that elephants could stand a breast and casually pass through hundreds at a time. The tiny threshold of my bar mitzvah was a child's door and this was the door of a king. Today was my coronation and I had received my birthright from my Heavenly parents and it was magnificent, more than the pyramids and temples of King Solomon and all the Pharaoh's combined. I dreamed this dream, I felt this dream. Even though it was bigger than any dream anyone had ever dreamed, even Caesar and Pilot and all the Pharaohs and queens had never dreamed this dream. This dream was my calling, my purpose, my memory before body to fulfill in body. God felt my heart, heard my mind and made my dream even more grandiose than I imagined it to be. My secret heart was never hidden from Source.

For in my service I had always struggled with the part of me that dreamed of being more than a servant. Only Source could make me understand that to rule as a King or Queen was to be forever in service to the people, a complete sacrifice of a simple personal life was the crown of rulers that the common people never wore. I was born a slave and yet my loving God saw the grandiose glory of my dreams and gave me a taste of only the sweetest nectar of being a ruler, the glory and the praise without the life of restriction, responsibility, and obligation. How great is my creator to offer this precious gift, this trivial boyish dream and to do it in my own country by my own people. I was in awe and overcome with gratitude to see my secret heart's desire laid out on a silver platter of freedom. An infant slave as Moses was raised to the heights of human exultation, like the shepherd David, raised to be king, I sang a song in my heart and my body danced in spontaneous joy.

Today we go to the temple to offer our hearts and minds to God. Today we go to the temple to connect with our Brothers and Sisters. Today we go to the temple to remember, to celebrate and to share in the Holy work of our Creator. Today we go to the temple to learn and to teach as we pass through our individual lessons in our personal development as enlightened men and woman of Love. And today I go to the temple to set my fate in stone. Today I go to the temple to stand up and speak the truth I have come to reveal to the people. Today I go to the temple to fulfill prophecy and my destiny. Today I go to unleash the gates of hell on those who would bring hell into God's Holy Temple. Oh that today could be some other day, and yet, I go.

Along the way travellers joined with us and we began to sing. We sang the simple songs and chants that united our steps in love and revelation of God's will in our lives and God's presence that keeps us on our path. We sang of history and glory. We sang of lessons and stories. We sang, we sang, we sang to God. And our hearts were lifted as more and more people came out of their homes and along their way to join us in revelation and rapture. As we drew close to the temple we could barely hear the noise from within for our joy in singing was so grand.

We passed through the first arch and each of us made our tribute and acknowledgement of entering the most Sacred and Holy dwelling of our Creator. We bowed our heads and lifted our hands and hearts to God in humility and service, in respect and gratitude we poured forth into our Holy home, the Temple of God, the one and only Source of all love and light.

And as my eyes began to focus on the sight within the walls of this most treasured Holy site I was overcome with revulsion. I could not move, not a step, not a breath. I stood like a statue and beheld my worst dream, the one that would wake me shaking and drenched in sweat and tears. Oh my God, the dream of all the vilest possibility, God's Holy Temple defiled by demons and the blackest filth of the devil's dream, greed; the same greed and competition that killed Able.

I felt the rage begin, the rage that would wake me from that dream in sweat and tears. The same rage that devastated Sodom and Gomorrah and the world in the flood. It began in my chest, my heart not just pounding but thrusting me in convulsions within the cells of my body. A heat that grew to such intensity that my heart felt like the heart of a mountain thundering and pounding as the liquid fire spews from its zenith. Not just my hands and feet trembling but my whole form from below my feet to above my head was ripped apart with heat and thunder. I saw in my mind's eye the white fire streaks that came from storm clouds that burned the ground and felt its power surging through me like the dragons of old time the fire that did not consume my body burst out of me from all angles; my mouth open and the fire spewing from me. I ravaged the scene, the people, my Father's Holy space.

I screamed of the atrocity of this violation and of the visions I saw in my dreams of massive metal Egyptian auk shaped flying things in the sky without the containing ring, the broken cross shaped demons that carried metal seeds of fire and destruction. I saw the seed that lands on the foreign people with slit shaped eyes and the bodies of men, women and children whose flesh is burned from their flailing forms to eradicate and poison the earth where they stood for generations. I saw the waving cloth with stars and stripes, crosses and hammers and sickles and colours of blue, red and white and yellow all waving in the wind as the blood rained down and drenched those icons of freedom into blood soaked visions of evil.

The fear and the lies of the nations who would use metal spears that shot metal balls of fire into their foreign brethren and leave the whole of the world decimated by fear and the brink of world devastation. I saw families gather in the depths of the earth in earthen, wooden, metal and stone rooms to hide from the onslaught of falling fire and liquid poisons that burn the flesh and lungs of those who breathe its noxious toxic death. I saw the people killing each other from little rooms with lights and metal magic seeing their brothers and sisters only from a viewing picture box from places of great distance, sending metal horror of fire to the farthest reaches of the world. I saw the entire world united not once but twice in war against each other like nothing the Egyptian pharaohs or Roman emperors could ever dream or enact. They enslave and destroy their own people to dig for gold and jewels and back liquid power. They kill and enslave to force entire countries to grow crops of controlling plants of the mind and hearts of fathers, mothers and children; killing the spirit as well as the body.

I saw in this one moment in the most Holy Temple of God the beginning of the next 2000 years of secrets and warfare of powerful people to enslave the world beyond any imagining and willing to kill leaders, children, forests, seas, the Earth itself to have more and more wealth and enslave more and more people. Everything that I was born for, freedom and love was twisted into a justification of all manner of evil in my name. And my name would be used to promote the Devil's service and my message of love would be lost to many as the people's fears, greed and competition would annihilate hope, freedom and love. The ones who would call me saviour, teacher and lord are the ones who will twist my words and kill their brothers, sisters and children of all colour, language, culture, religion, and country for their personal faith in God. They will bring world war, and create dark magic of mass destruction, burning crosses, burning books, burning souls for their fears, greed and competition.

Once again, before me stood the birth and desecration of my legacy and the vision of it broke me. And broken I raged and my body broken for them I raged at the seeds, the young ones who would carry on this travesty this perversion of Holiness and I could not weep I could only rage. I turned the tables of the businesses, I cursed them all, I screamed, I thrust my fist and my body to the ground and with thunder in my soul I raged and ravaged that broken Holy Sacred place of my Source, my Love, my God. All I did as I had done before, in the beginning of my time when this sight stirred me up inside unleashing the man in me. At the beginning of my time in my childhood home I raged through the Temple. God always gives mercy and grace to the first break. When consequences had me on the shoulders of murderously angry men to cast me to my death, God removed me safely and miraculously. And God counselled me of His Holy will for my brothers and sisters and their unfolding path of greed and power. God knew and I knew that moment of grace and mercy was a preparation for today. For I would know the consequences, death, that would befall me for repeating my broken-hearted rage on my family, the family I came to show the way back to the Kingdom of God, back to the love of our Father in heaven. And the only way for me to show them the Truth was to display the Truth in me and through me for all to see. I failed to hear the voice of Christ in me, blocking all that Holy Unconditional love out of my mind to fully immerse myself in the rage of the desecration of our Father's house. A rage born of fear of all that people would do in my name against God's Holy will to destroy this world and each other.

The first Temple cleanse was my lesson of preparation for the ultimate lesson of Perfection. I chose to demonstrate for my brothers and sisters about the consequences of sin and the Truth of atonement, forgiveness and rebirth. I came to choose this path of death and pain to show all people the power of personal creation and the responsibility of the creator to accept the blessings and the consequences peacefully and equally. As the following scene played out I was split in two between the Christ in me who loves all and the man who fears.

And in a blur of burning tears I saw their shocked faces and wide eyes of disbelief that I, the shepherd of love, meekness and forgiveness would unfurl all the fires of hell on them for this sacrilege. I saw those shocked broken faces and remembered bits of dreams and remembered bits of what was to come and as my strength began to wane I staggered to the entrance. I looked back at those faces to remember them all as I would see all those faces again very soon. All those faces would stand before me accusing me, condemning me. And I would be judged for all the truth and hell I brought forth on them today.

I slept the entire following day. I slept like the dead and could not be roused by anyone. My beloved sister and lover, Mary pressed her body to me and held me as I shook and trembled in this death like sleep. She washed my face of the sweat and loved me as only my beloved student and teacher, lover and friend and partner could. She was near me until I finally returned to this world renewed in my path to finish what I had begun since the day of my birth and every day and every moment, every thought and feeling and imagining of my beginning was unfolding in these final few days in Jerusalem.

Fear them not therefore: for there is nothing covered, that shall not be revealed; and hid, that shall not be known. (Matt 10:26)

BOOK 4

Seeds Of Freedom

And so as I lay there between worlds, my beloved comforted my fleshly self as my Spiritual being communed with my Source, my Heavenly Father. I needed to be renewed in my faith, restored to my path and returned to this world a willing, ready and worthy servant of Love's greater plan. I had been so depleted by the rage of the temple oscillating between guilt and justification. I sought unification of self or I would completely sever my being in twain and fall to oblivion of my own will and hand. The debate inside my being was intense, better to take my life than to give it to those who sought to use my life for global domination and terror. I would be forgotten then; no memory wants to hold onto a leader who gives up the battle. I could have left this world in peace, quietly privately of my own will rather than have my being ripped and torn asunder by those evil intentions.

As the cerebral serpent and I fought inside my head I kept returning to the one and only stable thought and feeling, Love. What would love do for those people both the schemers and the slaves? The schemers, slaves to power and competition, wanted me dead, they wanted to annihilate my message, my presence and my legacy and I in fear of the outcome was ready to hand it to them on a silver platter. Love would not give up; Love is not a fighter but a persistent calling, a whisper to unity that always presses forward and never back. I looked at the outcome if I were to end my mission on this day instead of in the days that followed. I knew my choice would determine the next evolution of humanity. I had been born to do this task, I had been trained to fulfill this purpose and I was ready to tread my path that was laid for me before the dawn of human intelligence, human freedom of choice, human self-awareness.

That first day was when the highest archangel descended to this world to begin this school, this game, the path of my purpose here. The day that angel separated self into the birth of the human Ego, with free will and the capacity to fear and thereby accept the illusion of being a separate self and being separate from Source, our God. The birth of ego was the creation and first interactions with the veil, an ignorance and fear that would become the teacher of Perfection to the brave and faithful. Now people would learn to seek and to find truth by trial and error. Choice would replace the pure instinctual natural surrender of all animals to the will of God, as Lucifer's contributions created the animal world in the image of control. Attachment would begin the human mind on a path of judgement that would create consequences and blessings based not merely on choices but also on the judgements of each choice.

This Divine game is the beginning of the evolution of people into separate beings, who believing the illusion of disconnection from each other and Source are able to learn Perfection and the power of surrender. Prodigal children are the players in this Divine game. Each Spirt in the presence of God chooses to leave God's home to be born into a body to feel separate, learn individually, and struggle to remember choosing to come to be perfected unto Christ. Each of us come to remember that God's Perfection is the only peace any person can and will ever know. In humility to remember who we are and where it all began. In remembering self, knowing self and actively becoming ready and willing to return to Source, our Creator. And the Creator of this Game which is the school of Christ so we can find the only path to freedom is as connected individuals, a family. Adam our father and brother came to roll the dice and make the first move. He chose the path of my Spirit brother Lucifer and the path of control, the path of laws and judgment, the path of the animal world, the natural man.

And then the day my sister, Eve, mother of all, met that first Ego, that man, that partner and was forever changed. She being the reaction to Adam's choice of control became the character of rebellion, which is the partner of the oppressor and controller. For every action there is an equal and opposite reaction. Adam's action to control gave birth to every rebellion that ever was and will be. Without a controller there can be no rebellion. Our Father gave free will so that we would learn Truth and humility and be equal with God by progress and practice. And Adam took free will and called it religion, law, government and Big Brother's birthright to protect or destroy by means of control the weaker, lesser, younger.

Eve, our Mother would stand in paradise brave and strong and chose based on, feelings of curiousity and self-determination to break the traditions of the Oppressor, to break the laws of control and ultimately create a new form of control, adversarial control and thereby become slaves to fear and curiosity. How could I betray all that our first human angels gave to the foundation of the Game, the School of Christ?

What they began in self-determination created the foundation of this world of control, conquest and competition, judgement and greed. I had to offer all the slaves that followed Adam and Eve a chance to be free of the consequences of their choosing by revealing that judgment is the real enemy of Truth. I came to demonstrate how to be free of the illusion of fear that condemned all people by their own personal power to create hell, their own personal power to forget and disown paradise, and our garden home of connection and equality, Earth. This school or game began with the fall of the pristine to the prisoner, children of the most high to slaves of each other and fear. My brothers and sisters needed me to come and show them their own power to be free of those consequences by embracing and returning to Love which is free of all judgement. We can create our world from that one and only Source of all power, parental Love. I would show them that I created my life before I was conceived. I would choose to stand in peace and silently accept the responsibility of my judgments that determined my choosing and my creating, in perfect love and truth, because I am the way, the truth and the life. I have acknowledged my own creatorship and instead of cowardly bowing out by my own hand, or blaming any other being, I will walk with my dignity and faith toward the torture and suffocation of my creation. I chose to come to die. I wrote the script and the mob volunteered to play the role I needed to complete my journey. For as Job created all that befell him and remained constant in his Love for God, so too will I accept the fate that I have created in my mind and cemented in feeling in this my Holy Temple body.

Who am I to condemn anyone? What would Love do? What will I do? I could take the poison or throw myself to the depths or I can rise up and offer myself as the sacrifice that the people sought in order to find some repose from the torment of guilt and fear that drives ambition. And so it was in that day of healing, my mind was healed, was united in a single purpose, the purpose of Love. And so it was that I would go and follow the steps of my dreams and offer myself to those schemers and in so doing undo their schemes completely. The schemers would then suffer the fate of their desires and my own people would wear the badge of the condemned for as long as their fear consumed them.

As it was written and will be, the first shall be last and the last shall be first. In my time the Gentiles were ready while the chosen children of God had empty lamps to offer. And even seeing those visions of what my followers will do in my name I saw the one and the many who would come after the age of water and secrets to the unveiling of all secrets. The one, who is perfect in wisdom, who will come to unveil all and everything that is only part truth will be set aside for Universal Truth until the conclusion of the Game. I saw the One and even in the rage and chaos I knew the only way for the people to prepare for the coming perfection was to go through hell first. The kingdom of heaven waits in the water bearer, the pristine logic that holds all perfect feeling outside self in balance revealing pure Truth to a world of chaos. The third person perspective will emerge born of empathy that allows emotions to be lessons in perfection instead of catalysts for suffering. The mind and heart examined, understood, and triumphed over to invite only Perfect thoughts that create Perfect feelings and Perfect peace on Earth and in the Game of Life which is the school of Christ. The Holy teachers will come and reveal pure unification and Spiritual advancement and make ready the people for the power that will be bestowed on the next age of human evolution; the age of the unification brothers and sisters and global communication. The pure of heart and meek will teach the world to create anew.

Every time I closed my eyes I saw those eyes and in those eyes of pure logic in balance with pure feeling I too was healed of the pain and tragedy that would befall the world for centuries of darkness. I saw the eyes that will also hold miracles beyond my understanding. The future was only dark for a time and then the light of new logic would begin to grow and spread and all that I had taught on hillsides and temples, deserts and doorways of the meek and mild bringers of the Dawn would come to pass. I will pave the way with my life to build the road where everyone, my people and all the nations of the world will realize their own personal power and responsibility. People will unite under a single banner for a thousand years of peace. I am ready and willing to die for that peace today, because I came to die so that all the world would know how to love, to create peace in Perfect Truth.

I awoke from this test renewed. I told my beloved I was ready to continue. And we began preparations for our Last Supper, the Passover with my brethren. Mary listened as she always does. She stopped me and held my head to her heart and in its pounding I fell to my knees in tears for I would see her suffer as no lover should ever suffer. She would be by my side whether I told her to go or no. There were no words or power that would keep her from me and I was in torment to know how she would suffer beside me feeling every pain in her own body as if my body and her body were one.

She was stronger than I was and stood tall with her soft long arms enveloping me in longsuffering love. She pressed my ear to her belly and raised my chin and with a gleam and a glow she said, "I will be with you but I will not be alone." Her eyes fell to her lower belly and she smiled and I felt for the first time since before my own birth a cosmic connection to another being I had not even met in the flesh. A child growing in her that was the unification of our bond in Spirit and body that would carry our blood and our path for generations to come. Even on this path of torment that would unfold in the next days I would stare into her eyes and down to that little person unfolding in her body and those two images would give me strength. My child and my beloved were my strength because each represented the most pure Love of Source, my completion and my creation, the mirror of God in my family.

The cycle of life was enduring, eternal and exquisite and I was blessed beyond all measure of blessings for my sufferings would open a door that would allow the Love of Source to continue the work of Love in this fleshly world. I was to be used and abused for a choice I made before I was even conceived and born. And I cemented this path in that workshop 21 years ago when I created the most dramatic creation a boy could create. Sometimes in a flash I see the vision of my creation and wish I could alter it, but in feeling it was cemented and built already. I have bound myself to this path here on Earth and the Master Creator will bind this same path in heaven; as it is written, as below so will be a held in tune above. The secrets of the next age will mask my truth and my light but many will hold the love I share, the love I offer and in personal sacrifice of self for that same love will allow some part of my truth to endure in spite of all the deceitful, fearful, religious and political leaders who twist the truth for personal glory and fearful competition. The children will be born in truth and will advance that truth forward in spite of their father's and mother's fears. Change is natural and death is change and with that change a new life is eternally reborn.

And so we gathered together at the home of one of our healed brothers discussing the coming feast and celebration. Each of us knew my time was growing short and there was much debate among my brothers as to how to undo what was to come. We were there all together when my brother, Judas, rejoined us. He had been absent from the sight of the others but even on that day in the temple when I completed the preparations of this coming challenge, I saw him in the shadows watching. He was torn and avoiding direct contact as he questioned my path more severely than any of my brethren. He stood and watched the hell I unleashed in the temple and I saw tears in his eyes as he watched and waited. As the adversary called me into question in his mind so that his heart judged me unto death.

After I rejoined my brethren we traveled to Bethany to prepare for the feast day and discus matters of the heart. He was quiet but he was there. And so as we were in the midst of discussing how the Creator will bless us for our doings in love for all people. How our gifts we offer to each brother and sister, how each blessing and healing we share in with another person is the same as if we were giving to the Creator. We are blessed not by people but by the Creator who uses people to bless us; she stepped forward. She, a young maid with trembling hands and moist eyes came to me. She slowly made her way to me through the looming large men. She came to me. She was a flower and an angel. When I saw her my heart fluttered and my body was alive with compassion. She sat perfect before me and said, "Master I am sent to offer you the Creator's blessed anointing, as you are royal in the eyes of God." Then with a bowed head she laid her treasure at my feet.

She was silent and gentle as she bowed before me and with the grace and ease of lady's maid servant she unlaced my sandals. When her soft hands held my feet I was a boy again, nervous and energized. She was so beautiful and perfect, I was in awe of her courage to follow her heart and offer her gift to me. She used the water and soft cloth to wash my feet and then poured forth exotic expense oil and massaged my feet. Her powerful thumbs deeply pressing into my under side of my feet making me swoon. I was released for a time from all pain and tension that my body had been storing since that day in the temple.

She eased my feet free of the knowledge of the path I was walking toward in every unfolding moment. I was raised up out of my body and floating above the room I saw my brothers. I saw that their faces were not serene as mine. I saw that they were confused, angry, and distraught to watch this tenderness. Even as I floated in bliss they were tormented in fear. She finished her healing and took the last of the ointment from the pure white bottle and poured its remaining drops over my head and I was instantly brought back into my body. I saw her face and she and I spoke without words for a time. She gathered her washing bowl and materials and silently as she came made her way back through the large and looming men with angry faces to where she belonged. My beloved touched my should and as I looked into her eyes dripping in tears I saw she understood the blessing. She saw the love and the grace and mercy of this royal gift and her pride in me was overflowing. She knew nothing of jealousies only tender mercies and love. She understood the magic that had just unfolded from the tender offerings of a young girl to a Master who faces death as Socrates faced the Hemlock. This moment seemed to last forever, as I still felt in a place of pure pleasure and perfection in front of a group of my closest brothers who were set in small rages over the same visual miracle.

They could only see the intimacy, money, and waste. They failed to see the blessings and gifts that the Creator offers to all of us in our time of need. In judgement they missed the blessing and the miracle and yet again I had to explain the flow of love is not according to their fearful understanding. The abundance of Eden never left the world; the world of men just stopped appreciating it, stopped seeing it and spent all thought in stealing it, controlling it, owning it and so lost it in their own selfish fearful hearts and minds. And he, the one from the shadows, my fearful brother most distraught more enraged and most verbal chastised the gift and finally set in his heart the plan he had been thinking since before we came to Jerusalem. Until this moment it was a perfect scribbling that could be blotted out and changed if he had let love undo his fear but in this connection between the young girl and me and the expensive perfumed oil he had marked it in his stone heart. His focus was now his path as surely as my path was cemented 21 years before in the workshop when I felt it more than I saw it. He felt it and it felt necessary and it felt justified and he felt compelled to do what he was born to do too.

And so I watched every moment like it was a cascade of golden sand glinting in the sun, mesmerized and enchanted by each word, face and connection. When you know time is short time is changed in the mind and perception becomes all powerful. I wanted to savour each of my brethren, remember their perfections and revel in their passions. I felt outside of them observing them for the last time. We gathered in the home of a passionate friend and prepared a table for royalty in perfect simplicity. Every cup and every tray and candle set out with pristine care. This table would be remembered for all time, captured in space and then held captive in the minds of the world.

My beloved sat beside me. We surrounded our place in the centre with my dedicated and passionate brothers and disciples of faith. We stood at the door welcoming them in and as my hand grasped each forearm and embraced I felt a stirring in my chest and throat. I held each one close and longer than I had ever done before since I knew not if I would ever feel that familiar flesh and smell those familiar smells again. I memorized each face and felt each face pondering me, curious and sensing the depth of these last moments together. When we sat there was silence. We all felt the heaviness of this night. Then he arrived. My brother who feared this night more deeply than all of us combined. The moment he stepped into our space the space was changed and a chill ran through everybody in the room. He was nervous, quickly making his way to each of us as if in a dream, not conscious of his body's doings. He flitted and attempted to raise the heavy cold blanket that we were under with trivial distractions.

Now that we were all present, we prepared to celebrate the feast of fathers. When I prayed over the bread inviting the Holy presence of God to open our eyes to the sacred act of consuming, I was consumed with my own coming death. My death would take the matter of this fleshly temple and transform it into the gardens of new life in plant and animal energy. As my breath and excretions have fed the world, soon my body would be added to the menu. The fluids that pass through my temple are the fluids that passed through all my faithful disciples. Blessing the wine and feeling the foundational magic that binds us all together here, breathing each other in, eating and drinking each other's blood and body. We were part of system of self renewal to maintain the material elements of the game without and within every player of the game. All my prayers, blessings and revelations of the scientific factual nature of Earth reality were completely lost on my brothers. My beloved Mary carrying another vessel of body and blood in her womb to be consumed sensed the Truth I was attempting to convey in these our last lessons together. Looking at their faces, I knew I was teaching the air since these children were centuries from this advanced connective knowledge of life.

Finally he stood before me. He passed over my beloved entirely as I am certain her repelling energy made it impossible for him to even approach her. She was transfixed in a cold stare on his every move and he never met her gaze once. He stood jittery and possessed of all manner of fearful voices before me. Then he just stood there staring into my eyes, lost, a shadow of his life patterns fell across his face. He reached for my arm and as we stood still I told him to get it over with Brother, it's already done.

He suddenly became aware of all the eyes focused on him full of curiousity and suspicion. He turned and left. And we continued with our feast of symbols and followed our Father's, Father's traditions. And again my mind betrayed as my words conveyed my preoccupation with my coming death. I showed the bread to all of them and we took bits of it together the same way we are bits of solid life patterns scattered to the wind. We are bits of matter and we are inside each other and we are alone too, never touching for the great gorge of blood flows between all the bits infinitely and eternally holding us in form. The matter changes form but it is all from Source as the blood sustains the body, the body obeys the blood formed of mind and controlled by heart. A symbol of our existence and our infinity, our individuality and our complete oneness they gazed in wonder of my words as these pictures were beyond their mind's imagining I let it go. When I held the wine, I poured only one glass and shared the rapture of unity and connection with my brothers and sisters. As this wine is the life blood of our feast, unifying us in a great body that is both a single cup of wine and the many droplets carried from cup to mouth and body to body passing through each body and unifying everybody in omniscient feeling connection. And we ate and shared and savoured our last meal together in this form.

After the feast we sang and then we traveled to the garden to commune with God in our natural space. The sky above vast and full of angels and messages of what is coming and the solid earth below to remind us we are on stage and the vastness watches us closely. I wanted to be with my brethren but not close. I wanted to know they were there but I needed to be with my own thoughts. I stepped away from the group bidding them to stay where they were and pray for me and remember me as I followed the Spirit up onto a small hill and talked with my Creator.

Night had just fallen and I fell too. On my knees I saw what I had done as a boy and what I would do as a man and I fell. "I am willing, my heart goes where you guide me and my mind belongs to you, Creator. Is there some other way, some simpler path that I could still be in the will of Love and not have to befall the tortures of my father? I will follow, I will follow, I will follow, and I only ask that you make the path straight, simple and abundant with grace and ease. Only let me know and see what I must to continue and keep me spell bound in your mercy." As the man in me sought escape the Christ sought the will of God, where the man's fears end, Christ's service to God's will begins.

I returned to my brothers and they were sleeping. I huffed and felt betrayed by their callous indifference to my torment and suffering as I await the judgement seat. I roused them and mocked them slightly and asked again that they supplicate for me. Show me I matter, show me I have made some difference in your life and you value me. And in my head I shouted, "Because tomorrow I will be gone."

Again I returned to pray and I asked for guidance from my own mentors and masters. Moses and Elijah came to me and their stories were retold me in an instant as I saw that my path was a continuation of theirs. I communed with them alone in the garden in a way I can never commune with any one of the flesh. Their voices were inside me and their being was around me and together with me we created a trinity of purpose. Logical steps to the path of perfection that began when Moses led my people to freedom and Elijah anointed those people with freedom and the message of truth. I would carry their mantel through the pain of torture through the blood of atonement the people would receive the example that is the path to freedom.

Again I returned to my brothers and they slept. I heard the footsteps that drew me to where they were. And as my brothers were stirred to life in an instant when the voice of a soldier said, "tell us which one is guilty." And Judas stepped from the soldiers of Rome to me. Peter jumped up and cut off the ear of the one who spoke. In a flash I had the bloody ear in my hand and I placed it to the head of the soldier and it was whole. I turned to my brothers and calmed them with wisdom and truth and they conceded and all fight was gone from their minds and hearts. They knew it was time and they followed the Spirit of passivity to allow the events to unfold as the Creator wills.

Judas stepped forward and kissed my cheek. He was cold, his lips, his eyes, his soul, cold like mortal death was already upon him and he was merely the moving carcass, a zombie of the will of fear. Nothing of my brother was in him anymore. He never moved just watched as the soldiers took me. My mind became like a white light that was impenetrable. I could see nothing outside the white light and nothing from outside that light could see me, the real me, not my body but my soul.

Surrounded by soldiers, the men who give their souls and bodies to violence and slavery because it gave a brief antidote for the pervasive fear that consumed their entire existence. To have the power of pain, freedoms, life and death over others can distract anyone from the lack of power over anything including self as a slave to the rulers who use brute base power to command others to their will. The entire system of soldiers is based and built on the fears of masses of people controlled by another fearful select minority of people. Those few, the rulers, are still slaves to base thoughts but they happen to understand a little more about the workings of the world then their fearful slave brothers. And here I was to have my fears revealed to the world by only those who could do it, slaves of fear. And these soldier slaves mocked me, spat on me and gambled over every moment of my torture and atonement. I felt only sad pity to watch them like an outsider watches a group of lions disassemble and devour a deer. They were beings of only instinct and submission to authority. They were as weak as children left alone to manage a hostile world without any of the compassionate instructions of life and experience.

As they dragged my body from place to place and set me up to be whipped again and again. I was reminded of another journey that seemed to last for days of agony. I left my current torture and debasement for brief moments to be flashed back to the journey to the stable of my birth; those traveling days of random restrictions that send jolts through my body, waking me, rousing me to action when the time was ripe. Like military drills practiced again and again stopping for a brief respite then back to drills and more drills to prepare me for the tunnel and the white light. Again the white light would take me for a while and the shouts of people and tear of my flesh in the bits of metal and stone woven into the braided whips many tails, rip, slash, again, white light, jostling journey in the womb of my mother with my father's spitting ranting railing tirades back to soldiers, father, bumps and falls and songs from sacred places, my mother's voice and white light.

They brought me first to Herod and the taunting continued and the whipping and my transitions between now, then and some other someplace. Herod is a puppet and fearfully sends me to Pilot to put the blame elsewhere and to enact deeds forbidden under Jewish law. Herod was afraid of me. He trembled when I raised my head and looked him in the eye. Most of my torture and beatings were because of men in a mad mob rage and the abject terror of Herod who spurned them on to greater disgrace. Herod was of high enough understanding to know that what I sought to teach all the people would make him obsolete. A man as fearful as Herod would do anything, even deceive and destroy his own people for profit. The lashings and taunting continued until everything went quiet and a soldier thrust a crown of thorns down onto my head, I felt a lunge in my body to the ground like having all the air expelled in a single breath. I staggered and fell.

My eyes went in and out of focus and I saw a small bowl in front of a crippled man in the crowd beyond and my mind's eye flashed back again to the moving pictures of my father's workshop before Passover. I was tied to the beams for insolence and receiving my lashings and tauntings as I was expected to do. And in silent torture I noticed the bowl of tiny finishing nails, tacks no deeper than a figure tip. I received a lash of the whip and the tongue and I went deeper into my imaginings for now I was tapping tiny little tack nails into my father's head, around the top like a crown in my mind. I could feel it, the hammer, and the bone being chipped and gutted to fit the thorn holes of this crown. Blood running down in rivulets around the skull like a veil of blood. And here it was and I could never have nailed those tacks to my father

I was too busy hanging onto the rope to keep him from killing me and Miriam. I only imagined doing that, I never actually did it and here it is and the last detail of my perfect creation is complete, for I created my crown of thorns the day before Passover 21 years ago.

When I came to Pilot the world tilted and I saw something extraordinary that only the perfect moment can reveal. When I entered Pilot was in hurried exchange with his wife, whisperings and hushed instructions. I looked up and I was face to face at about 15 feet distance with this woman and our minds connected and I heard a soft voice say, "Do not worry, all will be well" and a melodic ringing like soft angels in my ear. She smiled without moving her mouth and her eyes shone with radiance, wisdom and esteem. She wanted to make eye contact with me and felt honoured to share this brief moment.

Pilot was quiet. He seemed to be pondering his approach to this situation. He was curious about me from his eyes but still very much organizing the next few steps in the game. He spoke with me as if we were alone. He seemed open and candid, sincere and yet something was being withheld from my full view of this man's intentions. He played oblique and unbiased so well that his indifference was incongruent with his singular attention to the matter.

He asked the questions he was expected to ask and I gave the only answers they could understand. At least the only answers I believed the soldiers and political officers from Rome and the Jewish councils could understand. I believe I could have told the full enlightened truth to Pilot and he would not have been surprised at all. He would have astutely concurred and proceeded to outline the plans for its protection. Yes, protection that was what he was about, his purpose, his gifts and his political placement offered him the ability to protect the secrets that others were not ready to know, light keepers or illuminati.

They enacted a very theatrical event above the heads of all the masses of people who had come to see me crucified. Pilot symbolically washed his hands and let the mass decide to release a convicted murderer and send me to be crucified. I could barely stand under my own weight and by this time the heat of the day grew and without nourishment or sleep my whole body stumbled in the street. I saw the face of young girl, big eyes and tears hanging precariously from them afraid to fall but impossible to hide. When I fell she gave me a piece of her veil and cleaned my face and buried her own into its bloody soiled remains and sobbed, and I choked for a moment, not sure if this would be the end. And a man took hold of me and set me on my feet. He heaved up the cross bar and put it on his shoulder saying, "it would be my honour, Master, lean on me if you need to, I won't let you fall" The soldiers let him carry the beam for me. And I followed the white light, the soft voice of my mother singing and laid down my life. At the top of the hill were all the vertical poles. I lay down and let my arms fall open. I looked at the man with the hammer and the nail, I saw my father. I saw the nail and how he was angling it into that space below the line where I used to put the little nails from my coat, my precious nails that take away the pain, that block out all the noise and save me from the shame. As he thrust it into my wrists I moaned and my heart said, Thank you Creator, thank you for my nails.

And then they hoisted me up, up, up and I was above all the faces, like masks. I heard the voice in my head of my lost brother, Judas, crying, I saw the tree, the rope and the 20 pieces of silver and then silence until I saw them. My women and my mentors, my mother, my sister and my beloved all stood with faces turned to me, moist with tears but soft singing from their throats and faces at peace, eyes closed and deep in meditation and prayer. These women were joining me in their minds, healing and carrying some of the emotional weight so I could feel connected to them at all times. In those moments of trance with my women I was startled by the taunting voice beside me. He railed against me, mocking me and spitting at me. I looked at him in curiosity that one condemned as I would choose to attack in order to block out the guilt and fear of the actuality of his own life creation and consequences. What a strange fearful fellow and I pitied him quietly until another voice from my other side drew my attention. He was defending me, loving me and I saw in him a glow of understanding. I spoke to him and told him this day we are united in paradise. He smiled and we both knew we were free. Over the two or three days of slow suffocation

I would have his peaceful face to adore and share as we died together accepting of our creations in peace.

Perspective is a wholly wonderful thing but sorely missed without even knowing it in so many people. My everyday life, traveling and learning from near and distant masters had afforded me a wide and diverse perspective on life and wisdom. I stood apart from the ignorant teachers in Synagogue in their fearful bubble of ignorance; I read all and explored all truth from all Sources, never fearing knowledge and education in all its many forms. It is from this diversity that I was able to answer the questions of people so clearly and perfectly because diverse perspectives and empathy help to fill in the missing pieces. And yet in this moment on the cross perspective came like a revelation. I was looking down on the masses and my women and suddenly the moving pictures of my father's murder began to play out in my mind and I watched but it was different now. Everything was the same and yet completely different. I saw the edge of my sister's skirts and heard the sound that sent my heart to panic instinct and then BLAM. I came running like I had always imagined but when I came around the corner I was struck on the side of the head with a hammer. To think, to think, to think. I need air to think. I pull against the nails and take in a deep breath and relax so my feet can be pulled up away from the sharp carved edge of the foot plate and alternate between the sharp edge carved into my buttock's plate and feet plate, drawing pain and blood alternately between breaths. Pull, breath, think, relax, continuous pain, pull, breath, think, relax, continuous pain, remember, remember, remember, remember, remember.

My whole world fell out of focus and everything that I had come to know and believe for the last 21 years was suddenly spinning around in a blur of confusion. I was hit on the side of the head with a hammer. Why did I never remember that? Because since the day of the murder you have only shared the story once to Judas and you shared it how you saw it, not how you remembered it. How I saw it? How I saw it? I opened my eyes and I was looking down from the cross and suddenly I was in the vision and I was looking down on the actions. Someone was running deftly to the rope and lassoed around my Father's neck and sprinting to the hook and dangling and dangling and sobbing and crying and dangling. And I kept playing it over again and again and I noticed myself in the corner of the doorway, passed out and blood running down the side of my head. I am unconscious and I am watching like the way I used to watch my mother when I was in her body, I am floating above the events. I can see everything, like I could always see everything.

Who is hanging, my father is hanging. Then who is dangling? Who is dangling? Who is dangling? Mother, it is my mother, she came in the other door when he hit me with the hammer. Miriam is already unconscious from the throw and fall. Mother is the one running so fast, rope so slick, hanging so long, hanging so long, oh my mother, the blood dripping from her hands. His face is waiting for her to slip, his rage going to finally put an end to all this defiance. My mother is slipping, slipping, slipping his feet touching, his hands beginning to work the rope when suddenly the rope cuts clean through his neck and his body and head drop side by side one in a heap and the other bobbing rolling off to stillness.

Miriam, Miriam, Miriam, she is standing, she is looking, she is angry and he is dead. Mother falls and Miriam goes to her. Miriam tends to her, runs to me, tends to me, and back and forth until mother awakes and begins to pack up our life to begin another. We all died that day, even my little brother lying in the hay only feet away as a violent drama unfolded in his unconscious non-verbal infant world. Suddenly I remembered it was Miriam with the reigns driving the wagon, mother had never let Miriam drive before, and mother was wearing working gloves. Strange the way the picture takes shape so quickly once the veil is removed. The finer details came into focus, the bits that didn't fit when I was too emotionally and physically compromised to question anything at the time. And none of us spoke of it because I thought they knew I did it and would let me atone for it in my own way. And they thought I was unconscious and completely ignorant of what actually happened and chose to say nothing to me unless I asked. And I did ask Miriam, what did Mom do when she saw Dad? And she said, "She touched his face, a tear fell and she prayed for him."

After that day I never thought of it again until I confessed to Judas one night when we were into hours of wine and confessions. I did not know when I confessed to an act, it was an act I created only in my mind and not participated in at all. I never questioned the pounding in my head from the hammer, it seemed appropriate. And I had always healed so fast I never took note that my hands were completely unhurt while my mother hid her hands from my close inspection forever after that day. The pieces I had but could not understand where they fit until the light in the corner showed my body still while my spirit watched from above in the lights the powerful tragic play I had written.

Pull, breath, think, relax, continuous pain, pull, breath, think, relax continuous pain. I am looking down into Miriam's eyes. I see it in her eyes now. She sees it in mine and we both know she killed our father, not me and not my mother. She did it the way I can see thoughts and feel other people feelings. She moves things with her mind. I am struggling to breathe every moment is a constant struggle to breath. Pull, breath, think, relax, continuous pain, pull, breath, think, relax. I need to understand. My mind always searching for the answer, the understanding of the Creator's infinite wisdom and plan and I asked again and again in my heart out to the white light that had left when I began to remember that day. I didn't do it. Why am I here Lord, I didn't do it. I did not kill my father. I have been and I am willing to die for Love, but I didn't do it. I am innocent, where is the white light of protection? "My God, My God, why hast thou forsaken me?"

And the white light returned and flooded my soul with revelation. And I was soothed and I was again in communion with Love. And the voice that spoke was a woman's voice and she reminded me what I had told Judas only weeks ago. Thorns instead of roses; I had not physically murdered my father, but I did with every cell of my being, thought and feeling created the space for his murder that day before Passover. I imagined every detail and then reimagined every detail to make it perfect and complete as a summer day. And I am and was born to be a master creator like my parents before me and I created that day. My father's dark karma invited it to be, like a buyer he signed off on the project before he was even 12 years old. My mother's own karmic choices to break free of oppression as her forbearers did before, with war and violence and her own feeling and imaginings used her like a pawn in my play. My mother was willing to be a pawn but it was in the end my sister's own creation and powerful evolutionary thought/body/feeling existence that allowed her to not only break free of domination and abuse but to transcend the very laws that allow it to function in our reality at all. The Heavenly white light and gentle voice in perfect love and acceptance of what is said clearly, "You all created that moment. Every moment is the creation of many, so no one can claim innocence for everyone has thought a thought and backed it with a feeling and let it fly into the universe like a boomerang or a bomb. And yet we love you anyway."

I opened my eyes and the sky fell like night, the people changed. Suddenly the people felt awkward and out of place, like the energy that steamed them up into a mob-like frenzy had all leaked away suddenly and they were unsure how or why they were there. Shuffling and uncertain they looked to each other for comfort and understanding. And I felt the end come and I shouted out in my last breath, "IT IS FINISHED" and it was. The game was over for me and I had done my part with a willing heart. What I came to do I finished and now I was ready to rejoin my life from before this mission, this adventure, education and journey for Love. I was finally going home.

When I awoke it was to complete blackness and a voice that I could hear calling my name in a whisper in my head. I laid very still in the pitch blackness and heard only the faint voice not with my ears but with my mind. I sensed even though there was no noise that I was not alone. Flashes of the last week ran through my mind as I attempted to piece together what was happening and where I was and if I was alive or in some other reality. Sensing my mental activity the voice stopped repeating, "Issa, be calm, Issa be calm, Issa be calm". The voice now began to reveal visions in my mind. The picture was of two monks one at my head and one at my feet and they were sitting. They looked like statues because there was no breath and no movement even behind the closed eyes. After seeing this vision I scanned my body and I could feel hands on my feet and hands on my head and I knew that the voice that spoke was also one of the people touching me. The one at my head came into focus and I began to commune with that being in my mind. I shared my feelings of wonder and curiousity about this awakening. I shared my feelings of longing for my beloved, my mother and my sister. I shared my sense that my body was floating and being flooded with light colours all over and the coloured lights felt like tingling caresses over my wounds and thoughts. I was calm and I was safe and surprisingly I was alive.

The being at my head was repeating to me old lessons from my travels in youth to the wise men and their land, culture and people. I was to stop my breathing to almost nothing and received the air from my body cells that contain all things. I did as I was shown and the three of us joined our minds even more deeply as our bodies lost all form and distinction and became a three being individual in that cold dark tomb. These familiar feelings passed in and through me like waves. I was instantly transported back to the desert where my Earthly commission began in full. The preparation of that time without physical sustenance drew me closer to my Creator for all my needs fulfilled in Spirit to my body could maintain my life force energy through the vigorous process of mental, emotional and physical transformation and translation. As in the desert I could feel the energy of the Creator pulsing through the being at my head and into my body and down to the being at my feet and then back again in a cycle that kept restoring my broken body to wholeness again. I have no notion of the time only the feelings in my body and from my thoughts that lifted me out of cold and dark and into pure light.

Suddenly I was very alert, my eyes flashed open wide and I was full and overflowing in this healing pact. The two realized my mental sharpness immediately and spoke with their mouths for the first time ever since I awoke more than a day ago. The first being at my head said to me, "Arise Issa, for your children await your return. I am a healing monk sent to prepare you for your final curtain and blessings before you depart with us to your home, in the mountains where your mother brought you so long ago. My name is Ben-ji and this is Emon and we will guide you over the next steps to your freedom. Welcome back, Lord

Issa, Lord Jesus and Christ of your time. You have done perfectly and we honour you."

The sound of rock scraping rock and bits of light began to spill into the dark tomb. My eyes burned and slowly adjusted to this new sensation of light with my new body of light. The two monks laid out my pure white robes and helped me to dress before we emerged. The guard was on the ground, not asleep just unconscious. When I touched him I felt the powerful fear that possessed him causing him to fall unconscious when the rock began to roll away without any person touching it. Ben-ji explained that the same gift Miriam has is also why Emon was with us in the tomb. It was Emon's job to move the rock when the Master awoke and the time was perfect. Emon stayed at the tomb to let the people who would come know I was no longer inside but risen and gone to do the work of the Creator. Ben-ji helped me with his intense powerful healing energy to move naturally and freely again. With his help and instruction I was able to project my light body anywhere. I sent my body to walk with two of my brothers and talk with them about my resurrection. I visited many people with this light body projection and the help of Ben-ji.

The first people Ben-ji took me to see in person, not as a light projection, but me in the flesh was to a secret garden space with Pilot and his wife. When we entered she immediately embraced me and let her tears fall like rivers. She was so full of feeling it was overwhelming to be in her presence. She evoked in me such powerful energies I felt I might burst out of my new light body and become the sun. She was contagious and gregarious in her passions. Pilot the thinker stepped forward and grasped my arm as my sacred brothers have always done. He was in awe of this moment as much as we all were. He took us to a small grassy clearing and we all sat in a diamond, knees to knees in the soft grass. Pilot was opposite me and his wife was opposite Ben-ji.

Pilot explained all that had transpired behind the scenes. He had made such elaborate plans to compensate for any potential upsets that might have unfolded but did not. He was the one who had the tomb picked especially for this revelation. Its location was private and large and the tomb was brand new, never used and much larger than an average tomb would be to account for enough air for the three of us to breath even as shallow as we were breathing. He chose the guard, a nervous man who faints at the sight of any provocation. And he hired the apothecary to create a spiced medicinal tincture to be put into the vinegar that I drank from when I was thirsty. As he said this my mind remembered how my body felt warm, thick and numb after I drank the potion. It had to be placed in vinegar to mask the powerful medicines to help induce coma and death like paralysis.

After drinking the potion my mind worked more slowly and I was still up there battling with the situation of my father's death and how I had come to be a part of that drama. I had in fact realized just before unconsciousness that I was the master creator of his death and that others carried out what I had so meticulously and passionately created; and how my journey of the last day mirrored my vision and my creation to perfection. I did it, I created as God creates a day, a tree, a mountain or a bird and I did it so powerfully and perfectly. Then as a loving humble son I went to the Creator and willingly offered myself for retribution of my violent creation. The actions of my mother and sister who followed the instructions of my creation like drones in a mob would follow the energy wherever evil or fear may lead it. And the Creator forgave me and I forgave me and I was given a new life and a new path. The passage of birth death and rebirth on the grandest scale and stage the world had ever known.

Pilot explained that he and his wife were chosen to be a part of this grand play long before I returned to begin my ministry three and a half years ago. The illuminati are watchers and they watch the evolution of peoples all over the world. They help some and destroy others based on a science that fits the protocols of the moment. They, like me, could see beyond the façade of reality to the connections between thoughts, feelings and the individual worlds we live in simultaneously. They like many others have been waiting for me to prepare the way for the next evolution. The secrets they keep are for the protection of our world. For much power given to too many children would rip the world to pieces and that is not the plan of our Holy Father. And so when I was in the temple and I saw the devastation and death of so many in my name and was overcome with emotion, I was seeing a future that must be for people to grow and evolve until the time when my true message can be received by worthy adult Egos ready to be conscious creators of reality together and individually.

Pilot had prepared a way of my departure when the time was right. He explained that enough people must witness me before I go to begin my new life. My women would be sent after I leave along a different route to the same destination. I would talk and share with the people then in a climactic and dramatic gesture I would simply float away from one life and walk into my new life. The four of us sat quiet letting the flow of the Earth enter our bodies and minds and fill us full of light and understanding. We all had roles to play and each of us had come so far and seen so much to be sitting here in a garden at peace with all the world and ourselves. Our journey touches and continues to touch generations of human evolution until the completion of the game. We felt blessed to have been chosen and found worthy and ready to be who we were born to be. All that we had done was merely an expression of who we were and the actions were like a testimony to the will of our Ego that in love and light surrendered everything to be who we were born, called, chose and were chosen to be. Every word I spoke and every act I made was a reflection of the thoughts and feelings of who I am. And I am like all people a child of the Creator and as a child the only dream I ever dreamed passionately and consistently was to be like my Creator, my heavenly Father – Christ. And I am.

Pilot reassured me that my beloved would be delicately cared for in her travels with the young one inside listening and learning to take the lessons to the next generation. My mother will stay here for a time as is her role to play. And my sister will leave with me. When Pilot spoke of my sister, Miriam, I saw the flash of my out of body vision of Joseph's death. Pilot saw my expression change suddenly and asked what happened. I had slipped out of the high light circle we had created when my mind again witnessed such power and pain. I told Pilot of my sister Miriam's gift. He had praised me over and over and I thought wait until you meet my sister, for she has a power beyond anything I had ever seen. I told him, that if they crucified me for my message and my actions, for the Truth of my very being, what would they do to my sister, Miriam. Pilot in a very serious tone told me, "That is why your sister must go with you. She must be safe and protected by the light workers. She must reveal nothing and keep her power hidden. For even in the enlightened home we were going to live; there would still be a fear of her power that would destroy our peace and sanctuary. Jesus, I tell you sincerely, if anyone finds out what your sister can do before the time is right, they will burn her at the stake, behead her or worse."

Pilot and his wife bid us farewell reminding me that we will meet again in far distant lands, we will be together again. As I turned to leave, Pilot took my arm and with emotion looked into my face. "Your brother, Judas, he is dead." I saw a man truly broken by the sacrifice of my brother and with genuine compassion shared the hard news to me in unity. I looked to the ground a moment to compose myself and replied, "I know, I saw it on the cross, he was a good man, thank you Teacher." And we separated our arms and left to our separate realities once more.

The monk, Ben-ji and I went out of the garden blessed and ready to finish the scene. I met with my chosen students. I answered their questions according to their ability to understand and Pilot's admonishment to keep the sacred secrets for this is the time of the fish, silent, secret flowing existence that will eventually bring us to the next age, the age of unity, communication and connections. The age where I see those eyes, the eyes that shine like mine but are free to share and be because the world will finally be ready to accept their birthright and power safely in Mother's time. The world will no longer have a choice, evolve or die. Those who evolve will form the next pool of life from which we will draw out our next existence. Those who refuse to change will become like stone in mind and body. Like rock people who are incapable of choosing to change from within they will be weathered by change from the outside forces that carry the last evolution of the game. The rest of the players will sit in the judgement seat before the mirror of truth and all that they forgive will be forgiven and all they refuse to forgive will kill them by the same judgement in their hearts and minds. Change and love are the only real laws and commandments, everything else is negotiable.

Eventually it was time for me to rejoin my chosen apprentices and make the plan of resurrection for all people clear and easy for them to see with their own eyes and feel with their own hands what the power of the Creator can do with an open and willing heart. I was to be the prime example for all people to be creators and to create salvation, atonement and resurrection with their own minds, hearts and bodies. It was an exciting time for me, since I was free from my life mission that held me captive before my death. I felt like a child reborn and set free on the Earth with new insight and understanding.

My new being was completely absorbed with my life as a father. An indulgence I had no notion to give myself to before dying, but now, with my life's work complete, I would see and understand a new aspect of the Creator's personality. I would continue to grow, change and evolve as the being I was born to be. When I rose up before the multitudes, I saw in the faces of the people, hope. A hope I knew would last 2000 years until the Holy Mother would reveal the rest of my story. My story as it is given to the one who like me, has but one all-consuming desire, to know everything as the Creator knows everything, as Solomon asked to know everything and as our world is born to be. We are all born from and to become devouring beasts that over time taking in the wisdom of life energy from the body and blood of all ages to grow and evolve more vast, expansive, and curious to know more. I was the lamb for this time and the one who comes will be the lion, tamed of the hunger to control and compete. She will master only self and willingly lay down with me to become a lamb and teach all the world to serve and be free.

But when that which is perfect is come, then that which is in part shall be done away. (1 Corinthians 13:10)

BOOK 5

Conclusion And Resolution

So some time after I wrote this story I was cleaning a toilet of all things. A powerful revelation shook me to my knees which thankfully, I was already kneeling on to scrub the bottom of the toilet bowl. I had offered myself to God, Source, and the all-powerful infinite Creator of all existence and was given visions. I wrote what I saw and heard and did my best to stay completely detached from the story because it was not my story after all. It was the story of my hero, Jesus of Nazareth. Jesus is the only other life I ever examined with all my passion and being besides my own life. My life passion has been and continues to be, Know Thyself and Know Everything. And in the search to know me and everything I came face to face with my hero and was granted the gift of insight and revelation.

After I finished that story of my hero I left it to be what it was and needing it to be nothing more than what it was. I felt it and saw it and every part of it was a whole and separate identity from me but fully understood by me. And then on my knees cleaning that toilet in my father's home I saw the missing piece. A piece of me I had left behind in search of me. In that bathroom I said out loud in tears, "Oh my God, it IS my story!" I grabbed a pen and I wrote it all down as I am typing it out now I can still feel that moment when I realized that all those visions I saw and heard were the metaphors and symbols of my existence, of my entire life.

I suddenly felt very calm and peaceful. The story I wrote was my story through the lens of the life of Jesus the only other person I felt I compelled to understand as much as myself. In the act of telling my story I have been set free. I cannot tell you the specific names or places of any of the characters in my story who bore the title, Judas, Herod, priest, or Pilot, because these people are real people alive today working out their own salvation free from judgement from me. As co-creators of my story, I invited them to play those roles to teach me the lessons I came here to learn. Lessons I chose while I was still in the womb of my mother, listening, thinking, feeling and remembering. On an unconscious and non-verbal level through-out those 10 months of karma building in my mother's womb and my whole life of pattern building playing out to reveal my life story as it is today. Not only were there people who played those roles in my story, but I played the roles of Jesus, soldier, Judas, Herod, priest, Pilot, Peter, Mary and all the other roles in the stories of other people's lives. I was the hero and villain depending on who wrote me in and how they wanted me to fulfill their creations in me and through me for their learning, progress and evolution.

I have no one and nothing left to forgive, because I have been perfectly forgiven. Only when I forgave the Judas, Priest, Herod and Joe in me was I able to fully forgive those roles played by other people in my own life. I have made peace with my Judas, my Pharisees and Sadducees, my Herod and my own self and we are all forgiven in my mind. And what exists in my mind is the foundation of my whole life. Now like the history of Jesus that continued under the name of Issa in India, I continue under a new name. As God changed Jesus' name in his story at 30, so too did God change my name. And I have found the power in a name. And there is great power in names and naming. The name binds us to all that the name has lived and those shackles can become your own personal heaven or hell. Choose your freedom and free yourself.

My story, simply, there was a time when I was too busy learning to be living. And then suddenly I was living what I was learning. I too felt worshipped by many and despised by a few. I was isolated for most of my life and at the height of my journey to Jerusalem when I was thrust high into the sky in adulation; I threw myself down to the dirt in judgement of many. I scorned and I judged. I remember every detail of my court trial, the people I trusted and held in esteem who stood before me, that mocking Herod judge and others who said all manner of evil against me. And I stood there watched by those 12 jurors and a courtroom of people and they believed the lies and not me. I told the truth, simple, complete truth. I trusted police men, Crown attorneys, churchmen, and all those people who betrayed me and sacrificed me when I was 17 years old. I remember the moment in my father's kitchen as we were all waiting for the verdict. I remember the feeling inside me, when the lawyer said they found me guilty. I was a witness who spoke true. They believed the lies of the accused and labeled me the liar. I knew I was innocent by God's laws. And I knew I was innocent by man's laws, the laws that were the foundation of our entire legal system. But we are not judged only by man's laws, we are judged by the laws of a higher place, our minds and hearts of which God knows every detail.

Guilty, they found me, guilty and I was innocent and I told the truth and I was still found guilty. How can that be, in a just world, how can that be? When we look with our own eyes we see only the actions but not the thoughts and feelings that created those actions and the outcomes and realities of those actions. Even though I was innocent, I had feared that judgement and so fearing I read in Job 3:25, "that which I feared has come to be". So when I, in my mind only, I saw the knives in the North West corner of that kitchen of my childhood home and in my mind, like Stephen King's "Carrie" I saw them fly into the flesh of my tormentor and cut and stab and behead that human demon of my childhood, I felt it and I repeated it and thought about it again and again and again. But I never killed a man with my flesh only my mind and my heart.

I murdered him a million times in that kitchen and like a ghost he just kept on living in my world. And so I also came to realize that my thoughts and feelings were the foundation of the creation of the next horror of my life, the torture and trials of the Passion of the Christ. I walked those old musty court room halls and rooms surrounded by fearful beings who would sacrifice a young innocent girl to keep some secrets hidden from the world. What is the torture and murder of a young innocent lamb to save the many sinners of the world after all? A price, they believed was well worth their freedom from judgement and responsibility for their actions.

Why take responsibility, learn the lesson and make better choices, and create a pure and just system that works for the people. That takes time and work and personal exploration and forgiveness when it is so much easier to just sacrifice the nearest and most available lamb instead. This world has laws that seek to control masses, ignoring the individual nature of Earth reality, to create a system that slaughters innocence to protect that flawed and fallible system of justice that has none. And so they slaughtered me to keep the police station reputation, court room slavery, and city free to continue their fearful imperfect ways. But I knew even when the verdict came that it is better to face the truth now than later. And I forgave them because as it says in Matthew 10:26, "Fear them not therefore: for there is nothing covered, that shall not be revealed; and hid, that shall not be known".

And so it is when you have eyes to see and ears to hear that no person walks without revealing all that they think, feel and fear. They wear it like a badge of honour or a scarlet letter of defeat. No person can hide from the truth of their mind and heart because it is their reality and it cannot ever be hidden.

And over the last years of my freedom and my new name and new life I have found this verse, this consolation that has atoned me from my past imperfect thoughts and feelings! Corinthians 13:10, "But when that which is perfect is come, then that which is in part shall be done away." And when I forgave me and all the players who played their parts so perfectly in the play of my writing, of my life, I found perfection. When I look at them, hear them, feel them I see, hear and feel the beating of my over-flowing heart in perfect love for them for showing me the way to perfection. Only when you can look at the one who strikes you in the face and see that they are holding the script and your handwriting in the margin says, "slap character in the face" can you truly turn the other cheek and let that character finish what you have already written, get the beatings out of the way so you can create a better scene another day.

The body will heal instantly and the mind and feeling can either learn from it or like it enough to create some more beatings to endure for love of pain or the attention that pain gives us in sympathy and human concern. For humans do love to see other humans in pain, to identify with that pain and to solidify human notions that life is pain. But life is not pain, like Deepak Chopra said; "it is merely what we must go through sometimes to find truth". And the truth is that like Captain Kirk, all too often we like our pain, we need our pain. Our pain is familiar and when it is gone, we mourn the loss of our pain and do all our thinking and feeling to recreate those primitive Fall from Grace Pains of the two year olds who have defied their parents' wishes.

You see, if no one is ever allowed to point out your mistakes, you will never have the opportunity to learn from them and do better and live smarter, freer and more loving and peaceful life. Just like a stubborn two year old learns to hide mistakes rather than learn from them grows to suffer so much longer and more painful lessons than the child who confesses, "Yes, mother and father, I did that and I feel wrong for it, please help me think better and feel better". And the help we receive is often so much more peaceful and easy and the burden is lifted and the path is clear and learning is expanded with responsibility and maturity. If you refuse to see your mistakes then you are lost. If you refuse to see how you are the master creator of every pain and torture and loss in your life then you are lost. Only when you choose to create differently can you be resurrected into the New United Heaven and Earth. Then you are not lost but found for all eternity in grace and freedom.

Only from finding the thought that created the mistake that invited the betrayal, that forged the bounds of slavery and then forgiving that very thought and replacing it with a new way of thinking can transcendence happen. So long as there remains even a single mustard seed of blame of anything that has ever happened to you, you are lost. Blame was one of Adam's falls from Grace. In so doing he took on all the sin of the world and passed it down for millennia to the rest of the world. He blamed woman and we followed that path and created the imbalance of life on Earth today. From that blame women became the scapegoat for everything that was wrong with life on Earth. But then woman lied because of fear and was shamed by deceit and chose to live a life in fear and bondage to lies. And so from that time forward as woman lied and man blamed life on Earth was forever changed. And so in lies and blame we find the road to hell and when every person seeks truth and is only truth and blames no one then every person is free and the creation process of life and living will reflect that peaceful state of grace.

Amazing Grace, how sweet the sound, that saved someone like me. Someone of my own creation transcended into a forgiven angel of light. The only difference between who I was and who I am is my thoughts. Even though God changed my name the imprint of all the names I have carried is in every cell of my body and I am one being with many names. I am single minded and having a single eye, I can easily see that this body and world is only light reflected and refracted through the lens of my own thinking and feeling. That is the miracle in <u>A Course in Miracles</u>, that when a thought and feeling change the whole world shifts and is brand new.

With practise you can actually feel and see the ripples that a single thought empowered by feeling makes in Earth reality. The kingdom of Heaven is where it has always been, where Jesus told them it was 2000 years ago, in the palm of your hand. What will you create? What will your heaven look like when you take the pen in hand and write your story and it is all good, forgiven and perfect. I would love to see your heaven and as I am creating my own I watch with great anticipation of the glory you will be and create for me to share with you. Thank you for being you and co-creating this world with me. I love you more deeply than you will know until you learn to love you that deeply too.